KNOW -

AN INSIGHT TO THE BOOK OF PSALMS

M. PAULSON JOSHUA

Made with ♥ on the Notion Press Platform
www.notionpress.com

Contents

Contents

Contents

Contents

Contents

Contents

Introduction

The Psalms are a treasure of spiritual wisdom, awaiting patient disciples to explore them through a lifetime of study. Written by about six different authors between 1050 B.C. and 900 B.C., the book of Psalms is divided into five sections, each corresponding to one of the first five books of the Bible:

- Genesis – Beginning (Psalms 1 – 41): "When I consider your heavens, the work of your fingers, the moon and the stars, which you have set in place, what is mankind that you are mindful of them?" (Psalm 8).
- Exodus – Redemption (Psalms 42 – 72): "Hide your face from my sins and blot out all my iniquity. Create in me a pure heart, O God, and renew a steadfast spirit within me" (Psalm 51).
- Leviticus – Sanctuary (Psalms 73 – 89): "Blessed are those who dwell in your house; they are ever praising you" (Psalm 84).
- Numbers – Sojourn (Psalms 90 – 106): "Our days may come to seventy years, or eighty, if our strength endures; yet the best of them are but trouble and sorrow, for they quickly pass, and we fly away. Teach us to number our days, that we may gain a heart of wisdom" (Psalm 90).
- Deuteronomy – Word of God (Psalms 107 – 150): "Blessed are those whose ways are blameless, who walk according to the law of the LORD" (Psalm 119).

The Great Chapters
The Psalms highlight numerous themes about God and His relationship with us:

Greatness of God: The majesty and power of His voice (Psalm 29), the excellency of His Word (Psalm 119), the perfect revelation of God (Psalm 19), the perfect knowledge of man (Psalm 139), His faithfulness to Israel (Psalms 105, 106, 107), His sufferings for us (Psalms 22, 69), and His kingdom (Psalms 2, 24, 110).

God's Worthiness to Worship: For His sovereign creation (Psalms 8, 104), His kindness to rebellious Israel (Psalm 78), His care and providence (Psalms 145, 146, 147), His enduring mercy (Psalms 103, 136), and His call to worship with obedience (Psalms 95, 96).

Other Subjects: The blessings of those who fear the Lord (Psalm 34), the blessings of the righteous (Psalm 37), the blessing of those who dwell in the house of God (Psalm 84), the characters of those who dwell with God (Psalm 15), the futility of idols (Psalm 115), the song of love (Psalm 45), the prayer of Moses (Psalm 90), and the Messianic Psalms (Psalm 16).

The Messianic Psalms, in particular, include Psalms 2, 8, 16, 22, 23, 24, 40, 41, 45, 68, 69, 72, 89, 102, 110, and 118.

The Psalms, found in the Bible's Old Testament, were written by various authors, including King David, Asaph, the sons of Korah, Solomon, Moses, and others.

King David: Often referred to as the sweet psalmist of Israel. His Psalms express a wide range of emotions, from deep anguish and repentance to joy and praise, reflecting his experiences as a shepherd, warrior, and king.

Asaph: Asaph was a Levite appointed by David to lead worship in the tabernacle. Psalms (Psalm 50, 73–83) that focus on themes of worship, God's judgment, and the importance of righteousness.

The Sons of Korah: The descendants of Korah, who was a Levite from the tribe of Levi (Psalm 42–49, 84–85, 87–88) that emphasize themes of worship, trust in God, and longing for His presence.

Solomon: King Solomon, known for his wisdom, is believed to have authored a few Psalms (Psalm 72, 127) that focus on themes of kingship, wisdom, and the blessings of God.

Moses: Psalm 90 is attributed to Moses, the great leader of Israel, and reflects on the eternal nature of God and the brevity of human life.

This book begins with the life of a blessed man and ends with his worship.

PSALM 1
The Way of the Righteous and the Wicked

- What he does not do (v.1): "Blessed is the one who does not walk in step with the wicked or stand in the way that sinners take or sit in the company of mockers."
- What he does (v.2): "But whose delight is in the law of the LORD, and who meditates on his law day and night."
- What benefits does he have (v.3): "That person is like a tree planted by streams of water, which yields its fruit in season and whose leaf does not wither—whatever they do prospers."
- The end of the ungodly (v.4-6): "Not so the wicked! They are like chaff that the wind blows away. Therefore the wicked will not stand in the judgment, nor sinners in the assembly of the righteous. For the LORD watches over the way of the righteous, but the way of the wicked leads to destruction."

Psalm 1 emphasizes that individual salvation comes through the word of God, while Psalm 2 proclaims that the salvation of nations and their inheritance of the kingdom will be achieved through obedience to the Lord Jesus Christ.

PSALM 2
The Kingdom of Jesus Christ

- The words of man (v.1-3): "Why do the nations conspire and the peoples plot in vain? The kings of the earth rise up and the rulers band together against the LORD and against his anointed, saying, 'Let us break their chains and throw off their shackles.'"
- The words of Jehovah (v.4-6): "The One enthroned in heaven laughs; the Lord scoffs at them. He rebukes them in his anger and terrifies them in his wrath, saying, 'I have installed my king on Zion, my holy mountain.'"
- The words of Jesus Christ (v.7-9): "I will proclaim the LORD's decree: He said to me, 'You are my son; today I have become your father. Ask me, and I will make the nations your inheritance, the ends of the earth your possession. You will break them with a rod of iron; you will dash them to pieces like pottery.'"

David wrote this Psalm around 1000 B.C. Daniel interpreted a similar message in 600 B.C., emphasizing God's sovereignty (Daniel 4:24-25). Paul in A.D. 67 reaffirmed Jesus as God's Son (Hebrews 1:5-6), and Apostle John, in A.D. 96, described Jesus' ultimate victory (Revelation 19:14-16).

- The words of the Holy Spirit (v.10-12): "Therefore, you kings, be wise; be warned, you rulers of the earth. Serve the LORD with fear and celebrate his rule with trembling. Kiss his son, or he will be angry and your way will lead to your destruction, for his wrath can flare up in a moment. Blessed are all who take refuge in him."

Salvation comes only to those who trust in Him. In the Old Testament, "trust" is used 152 times and is equivalent to "faith" and "believe" in the New Testament. This trust involves taking refuge (Ruth 2:12), leaning on (Psalm 56:3), relying on (Psalm 22:8), and staying upon (Job 35:14).

Psalm 3
The Psalm of Morning

A psalm of David, written when he fled from his son Absalom.

- The Persecution (v.1-2): "LORD, how many are my foes! How many rise up against me! Many are saying of me, 'God will not deliver him.' Selah."
- The Protection (v.3-4): "But you, LORD, are a shield around me, my glory, the One who lifts my head high. I call out to the LORD, and he answers me from his holy mountain. Selah."
- The Peace (v.5-6): "I lie down and sleep; I wake again, because the LORD sustains me. I will not fear though tens of thousands fall on every side."
- The Prayer (v.7-8): "Arise, LORD! Deliver me, my God! Strike all my enemies on the jaw; break the teeth of the wicked. From the LORD comes deliverance. May your blessing be on your people. Selah."

PSALM 4
The Evening Prayer

- The God of Salvation (v.1-2): "Answer me when I call to you, my righteous God. Give me relief from my distress; have mercy on me and hear my prayer." David addresses the public, "How long will you people turn my glory into shame? How long will you love delusions and seek false gods? Selah."
- The God of Sanctification (v.3-5): "Know that the LORD has set apart his faithful servant for himself; the LORD hears when I call to him." David advises, "Tremble and do not sin; when you are on your beds, search your hearts and be silent. Offer the sacrifices of the righteous and trust in the LORD. Selah."
- The God of Satisfaction (v.6-8): "Let the light of your face shine on us. Fill my heart with joy when their grain and new wine abound. In peace I will lie down and sleep, for you alone, LORD, make me dwell in safety."

PSALM 5
Prayer for Guidance

- Who God Does Not Hear (v.4-6): "For you are not a God who is pleased with wickedness; with you, evil people are not welcome. The arrogant cannot stand in your presence. You hate all who do wrong; you destroy those who tell lies. The bloodthirsty and deceitful you, LORD, detest."
- David's Faith and Prayer (v.1-3, 8): "Listen to my words, LORD, consider my lament. Hear my cry for help, my King and my God, for to you I pray. In the morning, LORD, you hear my voice; in the morning I lay my requests before you and wait expectantly."
- God's Mercy and David's Worship (v.7, 11-12): "But I, by your great love, can come into your house; in reverence I bow down toward your holy temple. Let all who take refuge in you be glad; let them ever sing for joy. Spread your protection over them, that those who love your name may rejoice in you. Surely, LORD, you bless the righteous; you surround them with your favor as with a shield."

PSALM 6
A Prayer in Distress

- David's Plea (v.1-5): "LORD, do not rebuke me in your anger or discipline me in your wrath. Have mercy on me, LORD, for I am faint; heal me, LORD, for my bones are in agony. My soul is in deep anguish. How long, LORD, how long? Turn, LORD, and deliver me; save me because of your unfailing love. Among the dead no one proclaims your name. Who praises you from the grave?"
- David's Troubles (v.6-7): "I am worn out from my groaning. All night long I flood my bed with weeping and drench my couch with tears. My eyes grow weak with sorrow; they fail because of all my foes."
- David's Hope (v.8-10): "Away from me, all you who do evil, for the LORD has heard my weeping. The LORD has heard my cry for mercy; the LORD accepts my prayer. All my enemies will be overwhelmed with shame and anguish; they will turn back and suddenly be put to shame."

The Psalms present a rich tapestry of human experience and divine interaction. They span the emotional spectrum from distress to joy, providing a framework for understanding God's role in our lives and His unwavering faithfulness. The Psalms invite us to reflect, trust, worship, and find comfort in the assurance of God's presence and salvation.

PSALM 7
David's Prayer for Deliverance

1. David's Plea for Help
    1. O LORD my God, I trust in you: save me from those who persecute me, and rescue me.
    2. If you don't, they will tear my soul like a lion, ripping it apart, with no one to save me.
2. David Calls on God to Act: Arise, O LORD, in your anger; stand up against the rage of my enemies. Deliver the judgment you have commanded.
3. David's Confidence in God's Justice: The righteous God examines hearts and minds. My defense is from God, who saves the upright in heart.
4. God's Anger Towards the Wicked: God judges the righteous and is angry with the wicked every day. If they do not repent, He will sharpen His sword; He has bent His bow and made it ready. He has prepared His deadly weapons and His flaming arrows against the persecutors.
5. The Downfall of the Wicked: The wicked conceive evil, give birth to lies, and dig a pit only to fall into it themselves. Their mischief will return upon their own heads, and their violence will come down upon them.

6. David's Praise for God: I will praise the LORD for His righteousness and sing to the name of the LORD Most High.

• 9 •

PSALM 8
David – The Glory of God in Creation

1. The Majesty of God: O LORD, our Lord, how majestic is your name in all the earth! You have set your glory above the heavens.

2. God's Power Revealed in Children: Out of the mouths of infants, you have ordained praise because of your enemies, to silence the foe and the avenger.

3. The Splendor of God's Creation: When I consider the heavens, the work of your fingers, the moon and the stars which you have set in place.

4. The Honor of Humanity: What is man that you are mindful of him? You made him a little lower than the angels and crowned him with glory and honor. You made him ruler over the works of your hands; you put everything under his feet: all flocks and herds, and the animals of the wild, the birds of the sky, and the fish of the sea, all that swim the paths of the seas.

5. Closing Praise: O LORD, our Lord, how majestic is your name in all the earth!

Psalm 9

David – The Righteous Judgment of God

1. David's Praise to God: I will praise you, LORD, with all my heart; I will tell of all your wonderful deeds. I will be glad and rejoice in you; I will sing the praises of your name, O Most High.

2. David's Understanding of God's Judgment: For you have upheld my right and my cause, sitting enthroned as the righteous judge. You have rebuked the nations and destroyed the wicked; you have erased their name forever. The LORD reigns forever; He has established His throne for judgment. He rules the world in righteousness and judges the peoples with equity.

3. God as a Refuge for the Oppressed: The LORD is a refuge for the oppressed, a stronghold in times of trouble. Those who know your name trust in you, for you, LORD, have never forsaken those who seek you.

4. David's Prayer for Mercy: Have mercy on me, LORD; see how my enemies persecute me. Lift me up from the gates of death, that I may declare your praises in the gates of Daughter Zion and there rejoice in your salvation.

5. God's Judgment on the Wicked: The nations have fallen into the pit they have dug; their feet are caught in the net they have hidden. The LORD is known by His acts of justice; the wicked are ensnared by the work of their own hands.

•

PSALM 10

Hope in God's Deliverance from the Wicked

1. The Persecution of the Wicked: The wicked persecute the poor, boast about their desires, and bless the greedy, whom the LORD detests. Their mouth is full of cursing, deceit, and fraud; under their tongue is mischief and iniquity. They lie in ambush in the villages, secretly killing the innocent, their eyes watching for the helpless.

2. The Attitude of the Wicked Towards God: The wicked, in their arrogance, do not seek God; in all their thoughts, there is no room for God. Their ways are always prosperous; your laws are rejected by them; they sneer at all their enemies. They say to themselves, "Nothing will ever shake me." They think God has forgotten and will never see it.

3. The Prayer of the Righteous: Arise, LORD! Lift up your hand, O God. Do not forget the helpless. Break the arm of the wicked and evildoer; call them to account for their wickedness that would not otherwise be found out.

4. Confidence in God: The LORD is King forever and ever; the nations will perish from His land. You, LORD, hear the desire

of the afflicted; you encourage them, and you listen to their cry, defending the fatherless and the oppressed, so that mere earthly mortals will never again strike terror.

PSALM 11
David – Suffering of the Righteous

1. Trust in God Amid Suffering: In the LORD I take refuge. How then can you say to me: "Flee like a bird to your mountain"? For look, the wicked bend their bows; they set their arrows against the strings to shoot from the shadows at the upright in heart.

2. The Righteousness of God: The LORD is in His holy temple; the LORD is on His heavenly throne. He observes everyone on earth; His eyes examine them. The LORD examines the righteous, but the wicked, those who love violence, He hates with a passion. Upon the wicked, He will rain fiery coals and burning sulfur; a scorching wind will be their lot. For the LORD is righteous, He loves justice; the upright will see His face.

PSALM 12
David – Confidence of the Righteous

1. The Prayer of the Righteous: Help, LORD, for no one is faithful anymore; those who are loyal have vanished from the human race.

2. The Words of the Wicked: Everyone lies to their neighbor; they flatter with their lips but harbor deception in their hearts. They say, "By our tongues we will prevail; our lips will defend us—who is lord over us?"

3. The Words of God: "Because the poor are plundered and the needy groan, I will now arise," says the LORD. "I will protect them from those who malign them."

4. The Hope of the Righteous: You, LORD, will keep the needy safe and will protect us forever from the wicked, who freely strut about when what is vile is honored by the human race.

PSALM 13
David – Prayer and Hope

1. The Prayer of a Righteous Man: How long, LORD? Will you forget me forever? How long will you hide your face from me? How long must I wrestle with my thoughts and day after day have sorrow in my heart? How long will my enemy triumph over me? Look on me and answer, LORD my God. Give light to my eyes, or I will sleep in death, and my enemy will say, "I have overcome him," and my foes will rejoice when I fall.

2. Hope in the Lord: But I trust in your unfailing love; my heart rejoices in your salvation. I will sing the LORD's praise, for He has been good to me.

PSALM 14
David – The Wicked and the Righteous

1. The Foolish Wicked: The fool says in his heart, "There is no God." They are corrupt, their deeds are vile; there is no one who does good. The LORD looks down from heaven on all mankind to see if there are any who understand, any who seek God. All have turned away, all have become corrupt; there is no one who does good, not even one. They devour my people as though eating bread; they never call on the LORD.

2. The Hope of the Righteous: God is present in the company of the righteous. The plans of the poor are mocked, but the LORD is their refuge. Oh, that salvation for Israel would come out of Zion! When the LORD restores His people, let Jacob rejoice and Israel be glad!

PSALM 15
David – The Demands of God

Who Can Dwell with God?: LORD, who may dwell in your sacred tent? Who may live on your holy mountain? The one whose walk is blameless, who does what is righteous, who speaks the truth from their heart; whose tongue utters no slander, who does no wrong to a neighbor, and casts no slur on others; who despises a vile person but honors those who fear the LORD; who keeps an oath even when it hurts, and does not change their mind; who lends money to the poor without interest; who does not accept a bribe against the innocent. Whoever does these things will never be shaken.

PSALM 16
A Song of David

1. The Words of the Righteous: Keep me safe, my God, for in you I take refuge. I say to the LORD, "You are my Lord; apart from you, I have no good thing." The holy people in the land are the noble ones; in them, I delight. The LORD is my chosen portion and my cup; you hold my lot. The boundary lines have fallen for me in pleasant places; surely I have a delightful inheritance. I will praise the LORD, who counsels me; even at night my heart instructs me. I keep my eyes always on the LORD. With Him at my right hand, I will not be shaken.

2. The Hope of the Righteous: Therefore, my heart is glad, and my tongue rejoices; my body also will rest secure because you will not abandon me to the realm of the dead, nor will you let your faithful one see decay. You make known to me the path of life; you will fill me with joy in your presence, with eternal pleasures at your right hand.

PSALM 17
David's Prayer of a Righteous Man

This is a prayer of hope from a person with a pure heart.

- Not from deceitful lips (v.1).
- No evil found in the heart (v.3).
- Mouth does not speak wrongly (v.3).
- I have stayed away from evil by following your word (v.4).
- Guide my steps on your path (v.5).
- I will see your face (v.15).
- I will be satisfied when I awake in your likeness (v.15).

The Nature of the Wicked:

- They oppress me.
- They surround me at every step.
- They speak proudly.
- They watch me with hostile intent.
- They are like lions eager for prey, hiding in secret places.

The Portion of the Wicked:

- They live for this world, their bellies full of hidden treasures.
- They have many children and leave their wealth to them (v.14).

PSALM 18
David, the Servant of the LORD

David spoke these words to the LORD on the day the LORD saved him from all his enemies, including Saul.

David's Worship (v.2-5; 46-50):

- I love you, LORD, my strength.
- The LORD is my rock, fortress, and deliverer.
- My God, my strength, in whom I trust.
- My shield, the horn of my salvation, and my high tower.
- I call upon the LORD, who is worthy of praise.
- I am saved from my enemies.
- Death's sorrows surrounded me.
- Floods of ungodly men terrified me.
- Hell's sorrows surrounded me; death's traps ensnared me.
- The LORD lives; blessed be my rock, and let the God of my salvation be exalted.
- God avenges me, subdues the people under me.
- He delivers me from my enemies; you lift me above those who rise against me.
- Therefore, I will give thanks to you, LORD, among the nations and sing praises to your name.
- He gives great deliverance to his king and shows mercy to his anointed, to David and his descendants forever.

David's Prayer (v.6): In my distress, I called upon the LORD and cried to my God. He heard my voice from his temple, and my cry reached his ears.

The Prayer Changes Nature by God (v.7-15):

- The earth shook and trembled; the foundations of the hills moved because He was angry.
- Smoke went up from His nostrils, and fire from His mouth devoured; coals were kindled by it.
- He bowed the heavens and came down; darkness was under His feet.
- He rode on a cherub and flew, flying on the wings of the wind.
- He made darkness His secret place; His canopy around Him was dark waters and thick clouds of the skies.
- From the brightness before Him, His thick clouds passed, hailstones and coals of fire.
- The LORD thundered in the heavens; the Highest gave His voice with hailstones and coals of fire.
- He sent out arrows and scattered them; He shot lightning and discomfited them.
- The channels of waters were seen, and the foundations of the world were uncovered at Your rebuke, O LORD, at the blast of the breath of Your nostrils.

The Blessings (v.16-24; 29-45):

- He sent from above, took me, and drew me out of many waters.
- He delivered me from my strong enemy and those who hated me, for they were too strong for me.
- They confronted me in my calamity, but the LORD was my support.
- He brought me out into a spacious place; He delivered me because He delighted in me.
- The LORD rewarded me according to my righteousness.
- According to the cleanness of my hands, He repaid me.

- For I have kept the ways of the LORD and have not wickedly departed from my God.
- All His judgments were before me, and I did not put away His statutes from me.
- I was upright before Him and kept myself from iniquity.
- Therefore, the LORD has repaid me according to my righteousness, according to the cleanness of my hands in His sight.
- You light my lamp; the LORD my God brightens my darkness.
- With your help, I can run through a troop and leap over a wall.
- It is God who girds me with strength and makes my way perfect.
- He makes my feet like a deer's and sets me on high places.
- He trains my hands for war so that my arms can bend a bow of bronze.
- You have given me the shield of Your salvation; Your right hand holds me up, and Your gentleness makes me great.
- You enlarged my path under me so my feet did not slip.
- I pursued my enemies and overtook them; I did not turn back until they were destroyed.
- I wounded them so they could not rise; they fell under my feet.
- For You armed me with strength for battle; You subdued those who rose against me.
- You have given me the necks of my enemies so I could destroy those who hate me.
- They cried out, but there was no one to save them—even to the LORD, but He did not answer them.
- I beat them as fine as dust before the wind; I cast them out like dirt in the streets.
- You have delivered me from the strife of the people; You have made me the head of nations; a people I did not know shall serve me.
- As soon as they hear of me, they obey me; foreigners submit to me.
- Foreigners fade away and come trembling from their strongholds.

The Work of God (v.25-27; 30-31):

- With the merciful, You show Yourself merciful.
- With an upright man, You show Yourself upright.
- With the pure, You show Yourself pure; and with the devious, You show Yourself shrewd.
- You save the humble people but bring down the proud looks.
- As for God, His way is perfect.
- The word of the LORD is proven.
- He is a shield to all who trust in Him.

Psalm 19
David's Perfect Revelation of God

Witness of God: In His Creation (v.1-6)

- The heavens and the firmament display God's glorious handiwork.
- Every creation is brought forth by God's word (2 Timothy 3:16; Psalm 33:6).
- Each day and night, they speak and impart knowledge (Hebrews 4:12, 13).
- Their message transcends human language; their voice reaches all corners of the earth (Romans 1:20).
- Their proclamation extends throughout the world, revealing God's universal message.
- The sun, like a joyful bridegroom, radiates God's glory, filling the earth with His light.
- Its circuit encompasses the entire world, symbolizing the pervasive presence of God's glory (Luke 24:27; Acts 10:43).
- Nothing is hidden from its heat; God's light shines for all to see (John 8:12).

Witness of God: In His Word (v.7-14)

- The law of the Lord is perfect, refreshing the soul.

- His testimonies are reliable, making the simple wise (Psalm 119:129, 130).
- His statutes are right, bringing joy to the heart.
- His commandments are pure, enlightening the eyes (Psalm 111:7, 8).
- The fear of the Lord is pure and everlasting.
- His judgments are true and righteous.
- His Word is more precious than gold and sweeter than honey (Psalm 119:72, 103).
- By His Word, His servants are warned and instructed (Proverbs 1:23; Jeremiah 6:10; Ezekiel 3:17-20; 33:4, 5; 1 Corinthians 10:11; Colossians 1:28).
- Keeping His Word brings great reward (Hebrews 10:35; 11:26).

Prayer to the Lord, My Strength and Redeemer (v.12-14)

- Cleanse me from hidden faults.
- Keep me from willful sins; let them not rule over me.
- May the words of my mouth and the meditation of my heart be pleasing in Your sight, O Lord, my rock and my redeemer.

PSALM 20
David's Interceding Prayer for the Righteous

Interceding Prayer (v.1-5):

- The LORD hears you in times of trouble; He defends you.
- He sends help from His sanctuary and strengthens you from Zion.
- He remembers your offerings and accepts your sacrifices.
- May He grant you your heart's desires and fulfill all your plans.
- We rejoice in your salvation and set up banners in the name of our God.
- The LORD fulfills all your petitions.

Answer to Prayer (v.6-9):

- Now I know that the LORD saves His anointed; He hears him from His holy heaven with saving strength.
- Some trust in chariots and horses, but we trust in the name of the LORD our God.
- They are brought down and fallen, but we stand upright.
- Save us, LORD; let the king hear us when we call.

PSALM 21
David's Joy in God's Strength and Salvation

1. Reasons for Joy (v.2-6):

- You have given the king his heart's desire and have not withheld the request of his lips.
- You have blessed him with goodness and set a crown of pure gold on his head.
- He asked for life, and you gave it to him, even length of days forever.
- His glory is great in your salvation; honor and majesty are laid upon him.
- You have made him blessed forever and exceedingly glad with your presence.

2. The King's Trust in the LORD (v.8-10, 12):

- Your hand will find out all your enemies; your right hand will find those who hate you.
- You will make them like a fiery oven in your anger; the LORD will swallow them up in His wrath, and fire will devour them.

- Their descendants will be destroyed from the earth, and their seed from among men.
- You will make them turn their backs in defeat when you prepare your arrows against them.

3. The Sin of the Ungodly (v.11): They intended evil against you and devised wicked schemes, but they cannot succeed.

4. Worship (v.13): Be exalted, LORD, in your strength; we will sing and praise your power.

PSALM 22
Reflecting Jesus Christ, the Good Shepherd

Jesus' Prayer (v.1-21):

- Jesus cries out to God, feeling forsaken and distant, but gives glory to God's holiness.
- He remembers how God has delivered His people in the past.
- Despite being mocked and despised, Jesus trusts in God's help.
- He describes His suffering in vivid detail, including His physical and emotional anguish.
- He pleads with God for deliverance from His enemies and asks for His strength and salvation.
- Jesus acknowledges God's past faithfulness and prays for His continued presence and protection.

In the Church Age (v.22-26):

- Jesus declares God's name to His brethren in the congregation; He praises Him.
- All who fear the LORD are encouraged to praise and glorify Him.

- God does not despise the afflicted; He hears their cries and praises.
- Jesus vows to praise God in the great congregation and encourages others to do the same.
- The meek will eat and be satisfied, praising the LORD and finding eternal life.

In the Kingdom Age (v.27-31):

- All the ends of the earth will remember and turn to the LORD; all nations will worship Him.
- The kingdom belongs to the LORD, and He rules over all nations.
- All who go down to the dust will bow before Him.
- A seed shall serve Him, accounting to the LORD for a generation.
- People will come and declare His righteousness to future generations.

PSALM 23
David's Psalm: Jesus Christ, the Great Shepherd

The Lord as Shepherd (v.1-5):

- The Lord is my shepherd; I lack nothing because He provides.
- He gives me rest in green pastures and leads me beside still waters.
- He restores my soul and guides me on the right path.
- Even in the darkest valleys, I am not afraid, for He is with me.
- His presence and guidance comfort me.
- In the presence of my enemies, He prepares a table for me and anoints my head with oil.

Assurance of Future Hope (v.6):

- Goodness and mercy will follow me all the days of my life.
- I will dwell in the house of the Lord forever.

PSALM 24

David's Psalm: Jesus Christ, the Chief Shepherd

God's Sovereignty as Creator (v.1-2): The earth and everything in it belong to the Lord, for He founded it upon the seas and established it upon the waters.

Qualifications for Approaching God (v.3-6):

- Only those with clean hands and a pure heart, who do not worship idols or deceive others, can ascend the hill of the Lord and stand in His holy place.
- They will receive blessings and righteousness from the God of their salvation.
- This is the generation that seeks the Lord's face, O Jacob.

Jesus Christ as the King of Glory (v.8-10):

- Lift up your heads, O gates, and be lifted up, O everlasting doors, for the King of glory will come in.
- Who is this King of glory? The Lord strong and mighty, the Lord mighty in battle.
- He is the King of glory.

PSALM 25
David's Prayer and Blessings

Prayer (v.1-7):

- I lift up my soul to you, O Lord; I trust in you, my God.
- Let me not be ashamed, and let my enemies not triumph over me.
- Show me your ways, teach me your paths, and lead me in your truth.
- Remember your mercy and loving-kindness, and forgive my sins for your goodness' sake.

Character of God (v.8-14):

- God is good and upright; He teaches sinners and guides the meek.
- His paths are mercy and truth for those who keep His covenant.
- He pardons iniquity for His name's sake and teaches those who fear Him.
- The secret of the Lord is with those who fear Him, and He reveals His covenant to them.

Prayer of Hope (v.15-22):

- My eyes are always toward the Lord, who will deliver me from my troubles.
- Turn to me and have mercy, for I am desolate and afflicted.
- Consider my enemies and deliver me; let integrity and uprightness preserve me.

PSALM 26
David's Psalm: Prayer for Righteous Judgment

Prayer for Judgment (v.1-5):

- Judge me, O Lord, for I have walked in integrity and trusted in You.
- Examine and prove me, for I have kept Your loving-kindness and truth.
- I have not associated with the wicked or evildoers.

Separation from the Wicked (v.4-5, 10):

- I have avoided vain and deceitful people, not sitting with evildoers.
- Their hands are full of mischief and bribes.

Worship of the Righteous (v.6-8, 12):

- I will wash my hands in innocence and praise God's wondrous works.
- I love the Lord's house and the place where His honor dwells.

My foot stands on solid ground, and I will bless the Lord in the congregations.

PSALM 27
David's Psalm: The Work of Faith

Confidence in God (v.1-3, 5, 10):

- The Lord is my light and salvation; I have no reason to fear.
- Even if enemies surround me, my heart will not fear; I trust in the Lord's protection.
- In times of trouble, He will hide me in His pavilion and set me on a rock.
- Even if my parents forsake me, the Lord will take care of me.

The Work of the Wicked (v.2, 12):

- Enemies seek to devour me and spread falsehoods against me.
- False witnesses rise against me, breathing out cruelty.

Desire of the Righteous (v.4, 8, 11):

- I desire one thing above all: to dwell in the house of the Lord and behold His beauty.
- I seek to know His ways and be taught by Him.

Worship in Hope (v.6):

- I will lift my head above my enemies and offer sacrifices of joy in His tabernacle.

Encouragement (v.13, 14):

- I would have despaired if I didn't believe I would see the goodness of the Lord.
- I wait on the Lord, being of good courage, for He will strengthen my heart.

PSALM 28
David's Psalm: Worship of the Righteous

Prayer (v.1, 2):

- I cry to the Lord, my rock, and ask Him not to be silent.
- Hear my supplications, O Lord, and do not be silent toward me.

The Work and Destruction of the Wicked (v.3, 5):

- The wicked do not regard the works of the Lord and speak peace while plotting mischief.
- God will destroy them and not build them up; they will go down into the pit.

Glorifying God for His Blessings (v.6-9):

- Blessed be the Lord for hearing my supplications.
- He is my strength and shield; I trust in Him and am helped.
- He is the strength of His people and the saving strength of His anointed.

PSALM 29
David's Psalm: The Voice of God

The Power of God's Voice (v.3-9):

- The voice of the Lord is powerful, majestic, and breaks the cedars.
- It divides flames, shakes the wilderness, and makes the hinds calve.
- It reveals His glory and strength.

The Glory of God (v.1, 2, 10, 11):

- Give glory and strength to the Lord; worship Him in holiness and speak of His glory.
- In His temple, all proclaim His glory; He reigns forever.
- He gives strength and blesses His people with peace.

PSALM 30
David's Psalm: Dedication of the House

Thanksgiving (v.1-3):

- I will praise the Lord for lifting me up, healing me, and preserving my life.
- He brought my soul from the grave and kept me from going down to the pit.

Worship (v.4, 5):

- Sing to the Lord and give thanks at the remembrance of His holiness.
- His anger is temporary, but His favor brings life and joy.

Continued Worship (v.11, 12):

- He turned my mourning into dancing and clothed me with gladness.
- I will give thanks to the Lord forever.

Psalm 31
David's Psalm: Prayer of the Righteous

Prayer of the Righteous (v.1-8):

- I put my trust in the Lord; let me never be ashamed. Deliver me in Your righteousness.
- Be my strong rock, my fortress, and lead me and guide me for Your name's sake.
- Pull me out of the net they've laid for me; You are my strength.
- Have mercy on me, O Lord, for I am in trouble; my eyes and soul are consumed with grief.

The Troubles of the Righteous (v.9-13):

- My life is spent with grief and sighing; my strength fails, and I'm reproached among my enemies.
- I'm forgotten, like a dead man out of mind, and slandered by many.

The Surrendered Life of the Righteous (v.5, 7, 14-16):

- Into Your hand, I commit my spirit; You have redeemed me, O Lord God of truth.
- I will rejoice in Your mercy and trust in You, O Lord.

- My times are in Your hand; deliver me from my enemies and those who persecute me.

The End of the Wicked (v.17, 18):

- Let the wicked be ashamed and silent in the grave; let lying lips be put to silence.

The Hope of the Righteous in God (v.19-24):

- Oh, how great is Your goodness for those who fear You!
- You hide them in the secret of Your presence from the pride of man and keep them from strife.
- Blessed be the Lord, who has shown marvelous kindness; love the Lord, all His saints, and be of good courage.

PSALM 32

David's Psalm: The Blessed Man of Righteousness

The Blessed Man of Righteousness (v.1, 2):

- Blessed is the man whose transgressions are forgiven and whose sin is covered.
- Blessed is the man to whom the Lord does not impute iniquity and in whose spirit there is no guile.

Confession of Sin (v.3, 4):

- When I kept silent, my bones grew old through my groaning all day long.
- Your hand was heavy upon me; my vitality turned into drought.

Confession and Forgiveness (v.5, 6):

- I acknowledged my sin and did not hide my iniquity; I confessed to the Lord, and He forgave my sin.
- For this, let everyone who is godly pray to You in a time when You may be found.

The Word of God (v.8-11):

- God instructs and teaches us in the way we should go; He guides us with His eye.
- Do not be like the horse or mule, who have no understanding; many sorrows come to the wicked.

But those who trust in the Lord are surrounded by His mercy; be glad in the Lord, all you righteous!

Psalm 33
God the Creator

Greatness of God (v.1-5):

- Rejoice in the Lord, for praise is fitting for the upright.
- Praise Him with music and sing a new song to Him.
- His word is right, and His works are done in truth; He loves righteousness and justice.

Control Over Creation (v.6-12):

- By His word, the heavens and earth were made; He gathers the waters of the sea.
- Let all the earth fear the Lord; He spoke, and it was done, and His counsel stands forever.
- Blessed is the nation whose God is the Lord.

Observance of Humanity (v.13-17):

- The Lord looks from heaven upon all the inhabitants of the earth; He fashions their hearts alike.
- The king is not saved by his army, nor is a mighty man delivered by his strength.

Hope of the Righteous (v.18-22):

- The Lord's eye is on those who fear Him, hoping in His mercy.
- He delivers their souls and keeps them alive in famine; our soul waits for the Lord.

Let Your mercy, O Lord, be upon us, as we hope in You.

PSALM 34
David's Psalm: Praising the Lord

Praising the Lord (v.1-3):

- David praises the Lord at all times; His praise continually fills David's mouth.
- David's soul boasts in the Lord, and the humble rejoice.
- Magnify the Lord with David; let them exalt His name together.

Reasons to Praise God (v.3-10):

- David sought the Lord, and He delivered him from all his fears.
- Those who look to the Lord are enlightened and not ashamed.
- The poor man cried, and the Lord saved him out of all his troubles.
- The angel of the Lord encamps around those who fear Him and delivers them.
- Taste and see that the Lord is good; blessed is the man who trusts in Him.
- Those who fear the Lord lack no good thing.

The Fear of the Lord (v.14-15):

- Keep your tongue from evil and your lips from speaking deceit.

- Turn away from evil, do good, seek peace, and pursue it.

The Lord's Favor and Disfavor (v.16-22):

- The Lord's eyes are on the righteous, and His ears are open to their cries.
- The Lord is against evildoers, to cut off their remembrance from the earth.
- Many are the afflictions of the righteous, but the Lord delivers them from them all.
- The Lord redeems the souls of His servants, and none who trust in Him will be desolate.
-

PSALM 35
David's Psalm: Prayer

Prayer (v.1-6):

- David pleads with the Lord to contend with those who contend with him and fight against those who fight against him.
- He asks the Lord to take up arms and come to his aid against those who persecute him.
- David seeks confusion and shame for those who seek his soul, asking the Lord to pursue and persecute them.

The Wicked's Treatment of the Righteous (v.8, 11-12):

- The wicked have laid nets for the righteous without cause, rewarded evil for good, and rejoiced in the righteous' adversity.
- They have attacked the righteous without cause, tearing them apart with false accusations and mockery.

The Love of the Righteous (v.13-16, 20-21):

- Despite the wicked's treatment, the righteous have shown love, mourning and fasting for them when they were sick.
- The wicked speak deceitfully against the quiet in the land, opening their mouths wide against the righteous.

Prayer in Suffering (v.17-27):

- David asks the Lord to rescue his soul from destruction and not remain silent.
- He implores God to judge his cause and not let his enemies rejoice over him.
- David prays for the shame and dishonor of those who rejoice at his hurt.

The Few on the Righteous Side (v.27):

- Let those who favor David's righteous cause shout for joy and be glad, continually magnifying the Lord.

Thanksgiving (v.28):

- David vows to speak of the Lord's righteousness and praise all day long.

PSALM 36
The Wicked and God's Glory

he Acts of the Wicked (v.1-4):

- David observes the transgression of the wicked, noting their lack of fear of God.
- They flatter themselves until their iniquity becomes hateful.
- Their words are filled with iniquity and deceit; they no longer seek wisdom or goodness.
- The wicked devise mischief and set themselves on a path of evil without abhorring it.

The Glory of God (v.5-7):

- David praises the mercy, faithfulness, righteousness, and judgments of the Lord, which reach to the heavens and depths.
- The Lord preserves both man and beast, and His loving-kindness is excellent.

Those Who Trust in the Lord (v.8-10):

- Those who put their trust in the Lord will be abundantly satisfied with His blessings.

- They will drink from the river of His pleasures and find life and light in His presence.
- David asks the Lord to continue His loving-kindness and righteousness to those who know Him.

PSALM 37
David's Psalm: Righteousness and Wickedness

The Superiority of Righteousness (v.16):

- The little of a righteous person is better than the riches of many wicked.

Characteristics of the Righteous (Various Verses):

- Meek, righteous, good, blameless, upright.
- They trust in the Lord, do good, delight in Him, commit their ways to Him, rest in Him, wait patiently for Him, keep His ways, and feed on His faithfulness.
- They do not fret because of evildoers.

Blessings of the Righteous (Various Verses):

- They inherit the earth, delight in peace, are not ashamed in times of evil or famine, show mercy and give generously, and have blessed descendants.
- Their speech is filled with wisdom and justice.

God's Relation with the Righteous (Various Verses):

- He grants them the desires of their hearts, upholds them, knows their days, orders their steps, delights in their ways, does not forsake them, places His law in their hearts, and strengthens them in times of trouble.

Psalm 38
David's Remembrance Song

Appeal to God (v.1-10):

- David pleads for mercy from the Lord, asking not to be rebuked in wrath or chastened in displeasure.
- He describes his sufferings, feeling overwhelmed by God's arrows and the weight of his own sin.
- David's wounds are infected, and his physical and emotional state is deteriorating.

Reaction of Brethren (v.11-14, 19, 20):

- Despite David's suffering, his friends and family stand aloof, and his enemies seek to harm him.
- They speak mischievous things and devise deceit against him, but David remains silent like a deaf man.

Hope in God (v.15, 21, 22):

- David maintains hope in the Lord, believing that God will hear his cries and not forsake him.
- He asks God not to be far from him and to make haste to help him.

PSALM 39
David's Meditation on Mortality

Acknowledgement of Silence (v.9):

- David refrains from opening his mouth in the presence of God, indicating humility and submission.

Process of Regaining Strength through Prayer (v.12, 13):

- He prays for God to keep him from sinning and to guard his ways, especially concerning his speech.
- David resolves to meditate on the word of God, which stirs his heart and prompts him to speak with wisdom.

Self-Judgment and Surrender (v.4, 5, 6):

- David acknowledges his mortality and the brevity of life, recognizing the insignificance of humanity.
- He reflects on the fleeting nature of life, comparing it to a handbreadth and a passing shadow.
- Despite human busyness and accumulation of wealth, David understands that life is transient.

Remaining Hope and Prayer (v.7, 12):

- David expresses his hope in the Lord, waiting for divine intervention and guidance.
- He waits for the Lord's salvation, placing his trust in God's sovereignty.

PSALM 40
David's Song of Deliverance

Benefits of Patience (v.1-3):

- David extols the benefits of patiently waiting on the Lord, recounting how God heard his cries and delivered him from trouble.
- He describes God's actions of lifting him up, setting his feet on solid ground, and putting a new song of praise in his mouth.

Thoughts of God (v.4-5): David reflects on the thoughts of God, which are too numerous to count, emphasizing divine omniscience and care for humanity.

Prayer and Salvation (v.13-17):

- He prays for deliverance from trouble and asks God to make haste in helping him.
- David acknowledges God's salvation and righteousness, expressing his delight in following God's will.

PSALM 41
David's Reflection on Suffering and Blessings

Blessings for Consideration of the Poor (v.1-3): David pronounces blessings on those who consider the poor, promising deliverance, preservation, and blessing from the Lord.

David's Prayer and Sufferings (v.4-9):

- He pleads for mercy and healing from the Lord, confessing his sins and seeking redemption.
- David acknowledges God's favor and upholding of his integrity, even in the face of betrayal and suffering.

Betrayal and Suffering (v.10-12):

- David laments the betrayal of his enemies, including a trusted friend, who speak against him and wish for his demise.
- He describes the pain of betrayal and the evil disease afflicting him.

Psalm 42
Meditation of the Sons of Korah

Desire for God (v.1, 2):

- The psalmist compares their longing for God to a deer panting for water, expressing a deep thirst for the living God.
- Their soul yearns to appear before God and experience His presence.

Pain from Words of Enemies (v.3, 10):

- The psalmist's tears are constant as their enemies taunt them, questioning the presence and power of their God.
- The reproaches of their enemies feel like a sharp sword, causing deep emotional pain and distress.

Remembrance of Worship (v.4):

- Recalling past times of communal worship brings solace to the psalmist's soul.
- They reminisce about joining the multitude in joyful praise and celebration in the house of God.

Comfort and Hope (v.5, 11):

- The psalmist encourages themselves to find hope in God, despite feeling cast down and troubled.
- They believe that praising God will restore their countenance and recognize Him as their source of strength and salvation.

Prayer of Hope (v.6-9):

- Despite their distress, the psalmist remembers God from the distant lands of Jordan and Hermonites.
- They feel overwhelmed by the trials they face, likening their situation to deep waters and waves crashing over them.
- Yet, they trust that God will show His loving-kindness and that His presence will be with them day and night.
- They express their lament to God, questioning why they feel forgotten and mourning because of the oppression of their enemies.

PSALM 43
Prayer for Deliverance

Prayer of Righteousness and Hope (v.3):

- The psalmist seeks God's judgment and intervention against ungodly adversaries.
- They implore God to deliver them from deceitful and unjust individuals.
- Despite feeling abandoned and mourning due to oppression, the psalmist expresses hope in God's intervention.
- They ask for God's light and truth to lead them to His holy presence.

Comfort in God's Countenance (v.5):

- The psalmist questions their troubled soul, encouraging themselves to find hope in God.
- They express confidence that praising God will restore their countenance and acknowledge Him as their source of strength.

PSALM 44
Meditation of the Sons of Korah

Remembrance of God's Salvation (v.1-3):

- The psalmist recalls the historical acts of God, including driving out nations and establishing Israel, demonstrating His favor and power.

Trust in God Alone (v.6):

- The psalmist declares their reliance on God rather than human strength or weapons.
- They boast in God's name and faithfulness, acknowledging His role in their lives.

Faithfulness Amidst Trials (v.17): Despite suffering, the psalmist affirms their loyalty to God and adherence to His covenant.

God's Knowledge of the Heart (v.21): The psalmist acknowledges that God searches and knows the secrets of the heart, indicating His omniscience and discernment.

PSALM 45
A Song of Love

Celebration of Christ's Beauty and Kingship (v.1-3): The psalmist extols the beauty and majesty of Jesus Christ, acknowledging Him as the King of kings.

Jesus' Triumph and Kingdom (v.3-5, 6-8):

- The psalmist describes Jesus' victorious reign, symbolized by His teaching and righteous judgment.
- They affirm Jesus' eternal throne and righteous rule, contrasting it with earthly kingdoms.

The Role of the Church in Christ's Kingdom (v.9-13):

- The psalmist portrays the church as the queen, adorned in splendor, and called to worship Christ.
- Believers are urged to forsake worldly ties and embrace their identity as Christ's bride.

Israel's Role in the Kingdom (v.14-16): Israel, represented by virgins, is envisioned as companions of the church, bringing praise and honor to Christ.

Universal Worship of Christ (v.17): The psalmist proclaims that Christ's name will be praised and remembered throughout all generations.

PSALM 46
God the Refuge of His People by Sons of Korah

Safety in God's Protection (v.1-5, 11):

- The psalmist declares God as their refuge and strength, providing help in times of trouble.
- Despite chaos and upheaval, they express confidence in God's presence and protection.
- They envision a river that brings joy to the city of God, emphasizing God's unshakable support.

God's Sovereignty Over Nations (v.6-9):

- Amidst turmoil caused by raging nations, the psalmist affirms God's authority and ability to bring peace.
- They urge all to witness God's works and recognize His power to end conflicts and establish peace.

Exaltation of God (v.10): The psalmist calls for stillness and acknowledges God's supremacy, declaring His exaltation among the nations and on the earth.

PSALM 47

God, the Ruler of the Earth by Sons of Korah

Exaltation of God as King (v.2-5, 8-9):

- The psalmist celebrates God as the great King over all the earth, emphasizing His sovereignty and victory over nations.
- They anticipate God's reign and the gathering of peoples to worship Him.

Call to Worship (v.1, 6-7): All people are urged to clap, shout, and sing praises to God, recognizing His kingship and authority.

PSALM 48

The Glory of God in Zion by Sons of Korah

Hope in the Eternal Kingdom (v.1-2, 8):

- The psalmist praises God's greatness in the city of Zion, highlighting its significance as the dwelling place of the great King.
- They express confidence in God's eternal establishment of His kingdom.

God's Protection and Majesty (v.3-7):

- God's presence in Zion is described as a refuge and protection against enemies.
- The psalmist reflects on past victories and the awe-inspiring power of God's presence.

Call to Reflect and Rejoice (v.9-14):

- The psalmist encourages reflection on God's faithfulness and invites future generations to praise Him.
- They affirm God's guidance and provision, promising to follow Him faithfully.

PSALM 49

The Foolish and the Wise by sons of Korah

People who are honored but lack understanding are like fools. They:

- Trust in their wealth (v.6).
- Boast about their riches (v.6).
- Leave their wealth to others when they die (v.10).
- Think their homes will last forever (v.11).
- Name lands after themselves (v.11).
- Bless themselves (v.18).
- Receive praise from others for their success (v.18).

The result for them is:

- Death will consume them (v.14).
- Their beauty will decay in the grave (v.14).
- They can't take anything with them when they die (v.17).
- Their glory will disappear (v.17).
- They can't save anyone else (v.7).
- They are like animals that perish (v.12, 20).
- They will never see light again (v.19).

But for the upright who live faithfully:

- They are fearless in times of trouble (v.5; Revelation 2:10).
- They will rule in the morning (v.14; 2 Timothy 2:12).
- God will redeem them from the grave (v.15; John 5:24).
- God will take them to Himself (v.15; John 14:3).

Jesus said:

- "What profit is it if a man gains the whole world but loses his own soul?" (Mark 8:36-37).
- "A person's life doesn't consist in the abundance of possessions" (Luke 12:15).

Paul said:

- Be rich in good deeds, ready to give, willing to share (1 Timothy 6:17-19).
- Focus on things above, not on earthly things (Colossians 3:1-2).
- Live for eternity, not just for the present, because the present is temporary.
- Seek heavenly glory; our true treasures are spiritual and eternal.

PSALM 50

Psalm of Asaph – God the Righteous Judge

1. God's Call and Judgment

   - God calls out continuously (v.1).
   - He is the judge of all, using heaven and earth as witnesses (v.4, 6).
   - Everything in the world belongs to Him (v.7-13).
   - He deals with His people to reveal His salvation (v.23).
   - God has made a covenant with His people through sacrifice.
   - He gathers His saints to Himself.

1. Instructions for the Faithful

   - Offer thanksgiving to God (v.14).
   - Fulfill your vows to the Most High.
   - Call upon God in times of trouble, and He will deliver you (v.15).
   - Glorify God (v.23).

3. God's Judgment on the Wicked

- The wicked have no right to declare God's statutes or take His covenant in their mouth (v.16).
- God will tear them in pieces because:

  - They reject His instructions (v.17-20).
  - They cast His words behind them.
  - They consent with thieves and partake with adulterers.
  - They speak evil and deceive.
  - They speak against their brothers.

  - They forget God (v.22).

PSALM 51
Psalm of David - A Prayer for Cleansing

1. The condition of a sinner by birth (v.5)

I was shapen in iniquity; and in sin did my mother conceive me.

2. Our God's greatness to give salvation (v.1, 4).

- Having mercy and loving kindness.

- Multitude of mercies.

- He speaks justice.

- He judges clearly.

3. Punishment after doing the sin (v.8).

The bones which thou hast broken may rejoice

4. Repent about his sin (v.3).

- For I acknowledge my transgressions

- My sin is ever before me.

5. The confession before God (v.4)

- Against thee, thee only, have I sinned.

- Done this evil in thy sight.

6. Prayer matters.

i. **For a clean heart** – Create in me a clean heart, O God v.10. Wash me throughly from my iniquity and cleanse me from my sin. Purge me with hyssop, and I shall be clean: wash me, and I shall be whiter than snow (v.2, 7).

ii. **Remove my sins** – blot out my transgressions v.1. Hide thy face from my sins, and blot out all mine iniquities (v.9).

iii. **To obey the Holy Spirit** – and renew a right spirit within me (v.10).

iv. **Not to leave us** – Cast me not away from thy presence; and take not thy holy spirit from me (v.11).

v. **Have always the joy of salvation** – Restore unto me the joy of thy salvation; and uphold me with thy free spirit. Make me hear joy and gladness (v. 12,8).

vi. **Deliver from doing sin** – Deliver me from bloodguiltiness, O God, thou God of my salvation: and my tongue shall sing aloud of thy righteousness (v.14).

vii. **To praise God** – O Lord, open thou my lips; and my mouth shall show forth thy praise (v.15).

7. The demand of God.

i. **Broken heart** – The sacrifices of God are a broken spirit: a broken and a contrite heart, O God, thou wilt not despise (v.17).

ii. **Keep separation** – Do good in thy good pleasure unto Zion: build thou the walls of Jerusalem (v.18).

8. God will accept.

i. **Our righteous work** – Then shalt thou be pleased with the sacrifices of righteousness (v.19).

ii. **Our worship** – with burnt offering and whole burnt offering: then shall they offer bullocks upon thine altar (v.19).

Psalm 52

The End of the Wicked and the Peace of the Godly

1. Against Those Who Oppose God (v.1-5)

   - Why do you boast of evil, O mighty man?
   - Your tongue plots destruction, like a sharp razor, deceitfully.
   - You love evil more than good and lies more than speaking truth.
   - You love all words that devour, O deceitful tongue.
   - God will destroy you forever, uproot you from your home, and remove you from the land of the living.

1. The Righteous Response (v.6-7)

   - The righteous will see and fear, and laugh at him.
   - "Here is the man who did not make God his strength, but trusted in his abundant riches and strengthened himself in his wickedness."

3. David's Testimony (v.8-9)

- "But I am like a green olive tree in the house of God."
- "I trust in God's mercy forever and ever."
- "I will praise You forever for what You have done."
- "I will wait on Your name, for it is good before Your saints."

PSALM 53

Folly of the Godless, and God's Final Triumph

1. The Heart of a Fool (v.1)

    - The fool says in his heart, "There is no God."
    - They are corrupt and have committed abominable iniquity.
    - There is no one who does good.

1. God's View on the Wicked (v.2-4)

    - God looks down from heaven to see if anyone understands or seeks God.
    - Everyone has turned away and become corrupt; there is no one who does good, not even one.
    - Do the workers of iniquity have no knowledge? They devour my people as they eat bread and do not call upon God.

3. God's Judgment (v.5-6)

    - They were in great fear where no fear was.

- God scattered the bones of those who encamped against you.
- You put them to shame because God despised them.

4. Salvation of Israel (v.6)

- Oh, that the salvation of Israel would come out of Zion!
- When God brings back the captivity of His people, Jacob will rejoice and Israel will be glad.

PSALM 54

Psalm of David - Prayer for Vindication

1. Prayer (v.1-3)

   - Save me, O God, by Your name, and judge me by Your strength.
   - Hear my prayer, O God; listen to the words of my mouth.
   - For strangers have risen against me, and oppressors seek my life; they have not set God before them.

1. Hope (v.4-5)

   - Behold, God is my helper; the Lord is with those who uphold my soul.
   - He will repay my enemies for their evil. Cut them off in Your truth.

3. Worship (v.6-7)

   - I will freely sacrifice to You; I will praise Your name, O Lord, for it is good.
   - For He has delivered me out of all trouble, and my eyes have seen the defeat of my enemies.

PSALM 55
Psalm of David - Trust in God's Protection

1. Prayer and Trust (v.17, 23)

    ○ Evening, morning, and noon I will pray.
    ○ I will trust in You.
    ○ Cast your burden on the Lord, and He will sustain you; He will never permit the righteous to be moved.

1. Betrayal by Friends (v.13-14)

    ○ They were my close friends; we took sweet counsel together and walked to the house of God.

3. Enemies (v.3, 15, 19-21)

    ○ They bring trouble upon me and hate me in their wrath.
    ○ Wickedness is in their homes and among them; they do not repent or fear God.
    ○ They break peace and their words are like swords.

4. David's Distress (v.2, 4-6)

- ◦ I am restless and my heart is in pain.
- ◦ Fear, trembling, and horror have overwhelmed me.
- ◦ If I had wings like a dove, I would fly away and find rest.

PSALM 56
Trust in God Concerning the Treachery of Men

1. Cry for Mercy and Trust in God

   ◦ Be merciful to me, O God.
   ◦ When I am afraid, I will trust in You (v.4).
   ◦ In God, I will praise His word.
   ◦ I trust in God and will not fear what man can do to me.

1. The Enemy's Evil Works

   ◦ They oppress me daily (v.1-3, 5-6).
   ◦ My enemies seek to swallow me up daily; many fight against me, O Most High.
   ◦ They twist my words every day; all their thoughts are against me for evil.
   ◦ They gather together, hide themselves, and watch my steps, hoping to take my life.

3. Judgment on the Wicked

    - Will they escape by their wickedness?
    - In Your anger, O God, cast down the people (v.7).

4. Prayer of Hope

    - You keep track of my wanderings and collect my tears in Your bottle.
    - When I cry to You, my enemies will turn back; this I know because God is for me (v.9-13).
    - In God, I will praise His word; in the LORD, I will praise His word.
    - I have put my trust in God and will not be afraid of what man can do to me.
    - I will fulfill my vows to You, O God, and render praises to You.
    - For You have delivered my soul from death and will keep my feet from falling, so I may walk before God in the light of the living.

Psalm 57
Prayer for Rescue from Persecutors

1. Prayer with Hope

   ◦ Be merciful to me, O God, for I trust in You; in the shadow of Your wings, I find refuge until the calamities pass (v.1-3).
   ◦ I cry to God Most High, who fulfills His purpose for me.
   ◦ He will send from heaven and save me from those who seek to swallow me up.
   ◦ God will send forth His mercy and truth.

1. Sufferings from the Wicked

   ◦ My soul is among lions; I lie among those set on fire, whose teeth are spears and arrows, whose tongues are sharp swords (v.4, 6).
   ◦ They have prepared a net for my steps; my soul is bowed down. They have dug a pit before me.

3. Praising God

- Be exalted, O God, above the heavens; let Your glory be over all the earth (v.5, 7-11).
- My heart is steadfast, O God; I will sing and give praise.
- Awake, my glory; awake, psaltery and harp; I will awake early.
- I will praise You, O Lord, among the peoples; I will sing to You among the nations.
- For Your mercy reaches unto the heavens, and Your truth unto the clouds.
- Be exalted, O God, above the heavens; let Your glory be over all the earth.

PSALM 58
Judgment on the Wicked

1. The Wickedness of the Wicked

- They work wickedness in their hearts and deal out violence on the earth (v.1-5).
- From birth, they go astray, speaking lies.
- Their poison is like the poison of a serpent.

2. Judgment on the Wicked

- Break their teeth, O God; break out the fangs of the young lions (v.6-11).
- The righteous will rejoice when they see the vengeance.

PSALM 59

Prayer for Deliverance from Enemies

When Saul sent men to watch David's house to kill him.

1. Acts of the Wicked (v.1-7, 15)

- Workers of iniquity, bloody men.
- They lie in wait for my soul.
- The mighty gather against me, not because of my transgression or sin, O LORD.
- They return in the evening, making noise like dogs and circling the city.
- They spew out words with their mouths, swords are in their lips.
- They wander for food and grumble if they are not satisfied.

2. Praising God (v.16, 17)

- I will sing of Your power.
- I will sing aloud of Your mercy in the morning because You have been my defense and refuge in the day of my trouble.

- To You, O my strength, I will sing, for God is my defense and the God of my mercy.

PSALM 60
Urgent Prayer for the Restoration of God's Favor

1. Judgment of God on Israel in Tribulation (v.1-4)

- God, You have cast us off and scattered us; You have been displeased.
- You have made the earth tremble and broken it; heal its breaches for it shakes.
- You have shown Your people hard things and made us drink the wine of astonishment.
- You have given a banner to those who fear You, to be displayed because of the truth.

2. Deliverance of Israel After Tribulation (v.6-12)

- God will divide Shechem and measure out the valley of Succoth.
- Gilead, Manasseh, Ephraim, and Judah belong to Him.
- Moab is His washpot, over Edom He will cast His shoe, Philistia will shout in triumph.

- Who will lead me into the strong city? Who will bring me into Edom?
- God, who cast us off, will You not go out with our armies?
- Give us help from trouble, for vain is the help of man.
- Through God, we will do valiantly; He will tread down our enemies.

PSALM 61
Confidence in God's Protection

1. Prayer

- Hear my cry, O God; attend to my prayer.
- From the end of the earth, I will cry to You when my heart is overwhelmed; lead me to the rock that is higher than I.
- For You have been a shelter for me, a strong tower from the enemy.
- I will abide in Your tabernacle forever; I will trust in the covert of Your wings.

2. Worship

- For You, O God, have heard my vows; You have given me the heritage of those who fear Your name.
- You will prolong the king's life; his years will be as many generations.
- He shall abide before God forever; prepare mercy and truth to preserve him.
- So will I sing praise to Your name forever, that I may daily perform my vows.

PSALM 62
Confidence in God Alone

1. Trust in the Lord (v.8)

   ◦ Pour out your heart before Him; God is a refuge for us.

2. Wait Silently in God Alone (v.1, 5)

   ◦ My soul waits silently for God alone; from Him comes my salvation.
   ◦ He is my rock, salvation, defense, hope, glory, strength, and refuge (v.1, 2, 5-7).

3. Do Not (v.10)

   ◦ Trust in oppression.
   ◦ Hope in robbery.
   ◦ Set your heart on riches.

4. Power and Mercy Belong to God (v.11-12)

   ◦ Power belongs to God.
   ◦ Mercy belongs to the Lord.

PSALM 63
Thirsting for God

When David was in the wilderness of Judah.
  1. Looking unto God and Being Satisfied (v.1-8, 11)

- O God, You are my God; early will I seek You; my soul thirsts for You in a dry and thirsty land where there is no water.
- To see Your power and glory as I have seen You in the sanctuary.
- Because Your loving-kindness is better than life, my lips shall praise You.
- I will bless You while I live; I will lift up my hands in Your name.
- My soul shall be satisfied as with marrow and fatness; my mouth shall praise You with joyful lips.
- When I remember You on my bed and meditate on You in the night watches.
- Because You have been my help, in the shadow of Your wings, I will rejoice.
- My soul follows hard after You; Your right hand upholds me.
- The king shall rejoice in God; everyone who swears by Him shall glory.

  2. Judgment on the Wicked (v.9, 10)

- Those who seek to destroy my soul shall go into the lower parts of the earth.
- They shall fall by the sword and be a portion for foxes.
- The mouths of those who speak lies shall be stopped.

PSALM 64
Prayer for Deliverance from Enemies

1. Prayer for Deliverance from the Wicked (v.1-5)

- Hear my voice, O God, in my prayer; preserve my life from the fear of the enemy.
- Hide me from the secret counsel of the wicked, from the insurrection of the workers of iniquity.
- Who sharpen their tongues like swords and bend their bows to shoot their arrows, even bitter words.
- They shoot in secret at the perfect; they shoot suddenly and fear not.
- They encourage themselves in an evil matter; they talk of laying snares secretly, saying, "Who will see them?"

2. Hope of the Righteous (v.10)

- The righteous shall be glad in the LORD and shall trust in Him.
- All the upright in heart shall glory.

PSALM 65
Praise for God's Blessings

1. Blessing of Worshippers (v.1-4)

- Praise waits for You, O God, in Zion; to You shall the vow be performed.
- You who hear prayer, to You shall all flesh come.
- Our transgressions prevail against us, but You will purge them away.
- Blessed is the man You choose and cause to approach You, that he may dwell in Your courts.
- We shall be satisfied with the goodness of Your house, even of Your holy temple.

2. God Blesses the Earth (v.5-13)

By awesome deeds in righteousness, You answer us, O God of our salvation, the confidence of all the ends of the earth and of the far-off seas.

- By His strength, He established the mountains, being girded with power.
- He stills the noise of the seas, the noise of their waves, and the tumult of the peoples.

- Those who dwell in the farthest parts are afraid of Your signs; You make the outgoings of the morning and evening rejoice.
- You visit the earth and water it; You greatly enrich it with the river of God, which is full of water.
- You provide their grain, for so You have prepared it.
- You water its ridges abundantly, settle its furrows, and make it soft with showers; You bless its growth.
- You crown the year with Your goodness, and Your paths drip with abundance.
- They drop on the pastures of the wilderness, and the little hills rejoice on every side.
- The pastures are clothed with flocks; the valleys are covered with grain; they shout for joy, they also sing.

PSALM 66
For public worship

1. Worship (v.1-4, 8, 13-15)

- Make a joyful noise to God, all you lands.
- Sing forth the honor of His name; make His praise glorious.
- All the earth shall worship You and sing to You; they shall sing to Your name.
- Bless our God, you peoples, and make the voice of His praise to be heard.
- I will go into Your house with burnt offerings; I will pay You my vows,
- Which my lips have uttered and my mouth has spoken when I was in trouble.
- I will offer You burnt sacrifices of fat animals, with the sweet aroma of rams; I will offer bulls with goats.

2. Marvelous Work of God for His People (v.5-15)

- Come and see the works of God; He is awesome in His doing toward the sons of men.
- He turned the sea into dry land; they went through the river on foot; there we rejoiced in Him.
- He rules by His power forever; His eyes observe the nations; do not let the rebellious exalt themselves.

- He holds our soul in life and does not allow our feet to be moved.
- For You, O God, have tested us; You have refined us as silver is refined.
- You brought us into the net; You laid affliction on our backs.
- You have caused men to ride over our heads; we went through fire and through water, but You brought us out to rich fulfillment.

3. Testimony (v.16-20)

- Come and hear, all you who fear God, and I will declare what He has done for my soul.
- I cried to Him with my mouth, and He was extolled with my tongue.
- If I regard iniquity in my heart, the Lord will not hear.
- But certainly, God has heard me; He has attended to the voice of my prayer.
- Blessed be God, who has not turned away my prayer nor His mercy from me.

PSALM 67
Blessings of the Kingdom Age

1. Prayer for Blessing (v.1-2)

   - God be merciful unto us, and bless us; and cause His face to shine upon us.
   - That Your way may be known upon the earth, Your saving health among all nations.

2. Call to Praise (v.3-5)

   - Let the people praise You, O God; let all the people praise You.
   - Let the nations be glad and sing for joy: for You shall judge the people righteously, and govern the nations upon earth.
   - Let the people praise You, O God; let all the people praise You.

3. Blessings and Reverence (v.6-7)

   - Then shall the earth yield her increase; and God, even our own God, shall bless us.
   - God shall bless us; and all the ends of the earth shall fear Him.

PSALM 68
The God of Sinai and of the Sanctuary

1. The Coming of Jesus Christ to Armageddon (v.1-2)

Let God arise, let His enemies be scattered; let them also that hate Him flee before Him.

- As smoke is driven away, so drive them away: as wax melts before the fire, so let the wicked perish at the presence of God.

2. Deliverance of the Righteous (v.3-6)

But let the righteous be glad; let them rejoice before God: yea, let them exceedingly rejoice.

- Sing unto God, sing praises to His name: extol Him that rides upon the heavens by His name JAH, and rejoice before Him.
- A father of the fatherless, and a judge of the widows, is God in His holy habitation.
- God sets the solitary in families; He brings out those which are bound with chains: but the rebellious dwell in a dry land.

3. The Coming of Jesus on the Mount of Olives (v.7-8, 21-23, 30)

O God, when You went forth before Your people, when You marched through the wilderness; the earth shook, the heavens also dropped rain at the presence of God: Sinai itself was moved at the presence of God, the God of Israel.

- The Lord said, "I will bring again from Bashan, I will bring My people again from the depths of the sea."
- But God shall wound the head of His enemies, and the hairy scalp of such a one as goes on still in his trespasses.
- Scatter the people that delight in war.

4. Blessings of the Kingdom Age (v.9-20)

- You, O God, did send a plentiful rain, whereby You did confirm Your inheritance when it was weary.
- Your congregation has dwelt therein: You, O God, have prepared of Your goodness for the poor.
- The Lord gave the word: great was the company of those that published it.
- Blessed be the Lord, who daily loads us with benefits, even the God of our salvation. Selah.
- He that is our God is the God of salvation; and unto God the Lord belong the issues from death.

5. The Coming of Jesus Christ in His Throne in the Kingdom Age (v.24-34)

They have seen Your goings, O God; even the goings of my God, my King, in the sanctuary.

- The singers went before, the players on instruments followed after; among them were the damsels playing with timbrels.
- Bless God in the congregations, even the Lord, from the fountain of Israel.

- Because of Your temple at Jerusalem, kings shall bring presents unto You.
- Princes shall come out of Egypt; Ethiopia shall soon stretch out her hands unto God.
- Sing unto God, you kingdoms of the earth; O sing praises unto the Lord; Selah.
- To Him that rides upon the heavens of heavens, which were of old; lo, He does send out His voice, and that a mighty voice.
- The God of Israel is He that gives strength and power unto His people. Blessed be God.

PSALM 69
An Appeal for Deliverance from Persecution

1. The Sufferings of the Righteous (v.1-12)

- Save me, O God; for the waters are come in unto my soul.
- I sink in deep mire, where there is no standing: I come into deep waters, where the floods overflow me.
- I am weary of my crying: my throat is dry: my eyes fail while I wait for my God.
- They that hate me without a cause are more than the hairs of my head: they that would destroy me, being my enemies wrongfully, are mighty: then I restored that which I took not away.
- O God, You know my foolishness; and my sins are not hidden from You.
- Let not those that wait on You, O Lord GOD of hosts, be ashamed for my sake: let not those that seek You be confounded for my sake, O God of Israel.
- Because for Your sake I have borne reproach; shame has covered my face.

- ○ I have become a stranger unto my brethren, and an alien unto my mother's children.
- ○ For the zeal of Your house has eaten me up; and the reproaches of them that reproached You are fallen upon me.
- ○ When I wept, and chastened my soul with fasting, that was to my reproach.
- ○ I made sackcloth also my garment; and I became a proverb to them.
- ○ They that sit in the gate speak against me; and I was the song of the drunkards.

2. The Prayer of the Righteous (v.13-21)

But as for me, my prayer is unto You, O LORD, in an acceptable time: O God, in the multitude of Your mercy hear me, in the truth of Your salvation.

- Deliver me out of the mire, and let me not sink: let me be delivered from them that hate me, and out of the deep waters.
- Let not the water flood overflow me, neither let the deep swallow me up, nor let the pit shut her mouth upon me.
- Hear me, O LORD; for Your lovingkindness is good: turn unto me according to the multitude of Your tender mercies.
- And hide not Your face from Your servant; for I am in trouble: hear me speedily.
- Draw near unto my soul, and redeem it: deliver me because of my enemies.
- You have known my reproach, and my shame, and my dishonor: my adversaries are all before You.
- Reproach has broken my heart; and I am full of heaviness: I looked for someone to take pity, but there was none; and for comforters, but I found none.
- They gave me also gall for my meat; and in my thirst they gave me vinegar to drink.

3. Asking to Judge the Wicked (v.22-28)

- Let their table become a snare before them: and that which should have been for their welfare, let it become a trap.
- Let their eyes be darkened, that they see not; and make their loins continually to shake.
- Pour out Your indignation upon them, and let Your wrathful anger take hold of them.
- Let their habitation be desolate; and let none dwell in their tents.
- For they persecute him whom You have smitten; and they talk to the grief of those whom You have wounded.
- Add iniquity unto their iniquity: and let them not come into Your righteousness.
- Let them be blotted out of the book of the living, and not be written with the righteous.

4. Hope of the Righteous (v.29-36)

- But I am poor and sorrowful: let Your salvation, O God, set me up on high.
- I will praise the name of God with a song, and will magnify Him with thanksgiving.
- This also shall please the LORD better than an ox or bullock that has horns and hooves.
- The humble shall see this, and be glad: and your heart shall live that seek God.
- For the LORD hears the poor, and despises not His prisoners.
- Let heaven and earth praise Him, the seas, and everything that moves therein.
- For God will save Zion, and will build the cities of Judah: that they may dwell there, and have it in possession.
- The seed also of His servants shall inherit it: and they that love His name shall dwell therein.

PSALM 70
A Prayer for Deliverance

Prayer of the righteous.

1. Make haste, O God, to deliver me; make haste to help me, O LORD.
2. Let them be ashamed and confused that seek after my soul: let them be turned backward, and put to confusion, that desire my hurt.
3. Let them be turned back for a reward of their shame that says, Aha, aha.

Hope of the righteous.

1. Let all those that seek thee rejoice and be glad in thee: and let such as love thy salvation say continually, Let God be magnified.
2. But I am poor and needy: make haste unto me, O God: thou art my help and my deliverer; O LORD, make no tarrying.

PSALM 71
God the Rock of Salvation

1. The confident prayer of the righteous (v.1-9).

In You, Lord, I take refuge; let me never be put to shame.

In Your righteousness, deliver me and rescue me; listen to me and save me.

Be my rock of refuge, where I can always go; You have commanded my salvation, for You are my rock and my fortress.

Deliver me, my God, from the hand of the wicked, from the grasp of the unjust and cruel.

For You are my hope, Sovereign Lord; my trust since my youth.

From birth, I have relied on You; You brought me out of my mother's womb. I will always praise You.

I have become a sign to many; You are my strong refuge.

My mouth is filled with Your praise, declaring Your splendor all day long.

Do not cast me away when I am old; do not forsake me when my strength is gone.

2. The wicked speak against the righteous (v.10-12).

For my enemies speak against me; those who wait to kill me conspire together.

They say, "God has forsaken him; pursue him and seize him, for no one will rescue him."

God, do not be far from me; my God, come quickly to help me.

3. The wicked will be ashamed (v.13).

May my accusers perish in shame; may those who want to harm me be covered with scorn and disgrace.

4. The hope of the righteous (v.14-21).

- As for me, I will always have hope; I will praise You more and more.
- My mouth will tell of Your righteous deeds, of Your saving acts all day long—though I know not how to relate them all.
- I will come and proclaim Your mighty acts, Sovereign Lord; I will proclaim Your righteous deeds, Yours alone.
- Since my youth, God, You have taught me, and to this day I declare Your marvelous deeds.
- Even when I am old and gray, do not forsake me, my God, till I declare Your power to the next generation, Your mighty acts to all who are to come.
- Your righteousness, God, reaches to the heavens, You who have done great things. Who is like You, God?
- Though You have made me see troubles, many and bitter, You will restore my life again; from the depths of the earth, You will again bring me up. You will increase my honor and comfort me once more.

5. The righteous praise God (v.22-24).

- I will praise You with the harp for Your faithfulness, my God; I will sing praise to You with the lyre, Holy One of Israel.
- My lips will shout for joy when I sing praise to You—I whom You have delivered.

- My tongue will tell of Your righteous acts all day long, for those who wanted to harm me have been put to shame and confusion.

PSALM 72

Solomon - The Reign of the Righteous King

The prophecy of the coming kingdom of Jesus Christ.
   1. Righteousness will be blessed (v.1-7).

- Endow the king with Your justice, God, the royal son with Your righteousness.
- May he judge Your people in righteousness, Your afflicted ones with justice.
- May the mountains bring prosperity to the people, the hills the fruit of righteousness.
- May he defend the afflicted among the people and save the children of the needy; may he crush the oppressor.
- May he endure as long as the sun, as long as the moon, through all generations.
- May he be like rain falling on a mown field, like showers watering the earth.
- In his days may the righteous flourish and prosperity abound till the moon is no more.

   2. All nations will surrender to Him (v.8-11).

- May he rule from sea to sea and from the River to the ends of the earth.

- May the desert tribes bow before him and his enemies lick the dust.
- May the kings of Tarshish and of distant shores bring tribute to him. May the kings of Sheba and Seba present him gifts.
- May all kings bow down to him and all nations serve him.

3. All the poor in the world will be delivered (v.12-14).

- For he will deliver the needy who cry out, the afflicted who have no one to help.
- He will take pity on the weak and the needy and save the needy from death.
- He will rescue them from oppression and violence, for precious is their blood in his sight.

4. All will worship and give glory only to Him (v.15-19).

- Long may he live! May gold from Sheba be given him. May people ever pray for him and bless him all day long.
- May grain abound throughout the land; on the tops of the hills may it sway. May the crops flourish like Lebanon and thrive like the grass of the field.
- May his name endure forever; may it continue as long as the sun. Then all nations will be blessed through him, and they will call him blessed.
- Praise be to the Lord God, the God of Israel, who alone does marvelous deeds.
- Praise be to His glorious name forever; may the whole earth be filled with His glory. Amen and Amen.

PSALM 73
Psalm of Asaph - The Prosperity of the Wicked

The tragedy of the wicked and the blessedness of trust in God.
God is truly good to Israel, especially to those with pure hearts.
1. These are the ungodly (v.1-12).

- I envied the arrogant when I saw the prosperity of the wicked.
- For they have no struggles; their bodies are healthy and strong.
- They are free from common human burdens; they are not plagued by human ills.
- Therefore pride is their necklace; they clothe themselves with violence.
- From their callous hearts comes iniquity; their evil imaginations have no limits.
- They scoff, and speak with malice; with arrogance they threaten oppression.
- Their mouths lay claim to heaven, and their tongues take possession of the earth.
- Therefore their people turn to them and drink up waters in abundance.

- They say, "How would God know? Does the Most High know anything?"
- This is what the wicked are like—always free of care, they go on amassing wealth.

2. Their end (v.18-20, 27).

- Surely you place them on slippery ground; you cast them down to ruin.
- How suddenly they are destroyed, completely swept away by terrors!
- As a dream when one awakes, so when you arise, Lord, you will despise them as fantasies.
- Those who are far from you will perish; you destroy all who are unfaithful to you.

3. The sufferings of the righteous and his end (v.13, 14, 23-28).

- Surely in vain I have kept my heart pure and have washed my hands in innocence.
- All day long I have been afflicted, and every morning brings new punishments.
- Yet I am always with you; you hold me by my right hand.
- You guide me with your counsel, and afterward you will take me into glory.
- Whom have I in heaven but you? And earth has nothing I desire besides you.
- My flesh and my heart may fail, but God is the strength of my heart and my portion forever.
- Those who are far from you will perish; you destroy all who are unfaithful to you.
- But as for me, it is good to be near God. I have made the Sovereign Lord my refuge; I will tell of all your deeds.

Psalm 74

A Plea for God to Remember His Covenant

1. Cry for Help and Divine Intervention (Verses 1-3):
We start by asking God why He seems angry with us, His people. Remember us, God, the ones You bought and chose as Your own. Think about Mount Zion, where You used to live.

2. Description of the Destruction (Verses 4-8):
Our enemies have caused chaos where we used to meet with You. They've put up their flags in our holy places. They've acted like lumberjacks chopping down trees.

3. Lament over the Absence of Signs and Prophets (Verses 9-11):
We're not seeing any miracles from God anymore. There are no prophets to guide us, and we don't know how much longer this will go on.

4. Recollection of God's Past Mighty Deeds (Verses 12-17):
But we remember, God, how powerful You are. You've saved us in the past. You parted the sea, and You defeated mighty monsters.

5. Plea for God to Defend His Cause (Verses 18-23):
Please, God, don't forget us. Our enemies are mocking You, and we're suffering. Remember us, Lord, and protect us from our enemies.

This psalm reminds us to trust in God, even when things look bad. We remember His past acts of saving power and pray for His help in our current troubles. We know that God is always with us, even in our hardest times.

PSALM 75

Praise and Thanksgiving to God

1. Praise and Thanksgiving to God (Verse 1):
We thank You, God, for being near us and for all the amazing things You do.

2. God's Declaration of Judgment (Verses 2-3):
You say, "I choose when it's time for judgment, and I keep things steady even when everything seems shaky."

3. Warning to the Proud (Verses 4-5):
To those who are too proud and wicked, I say, "Stop boasting and acting defiantly against God."

4. God as the Righteous Judge (Verses 6-8):
Promotion and power come from God, not from people. He judges fairly, bringing down some and lifting up others.

5. Affirmation of Eternal Praise and Judgment (Verses 9-10):
I will always declare Your praises and sing to You, God. You promise to punish the wicked and lift up the righteous.

PSALM 76
God's Power and Victory Over Enemies

1. God's Presence and Greatness (Verses 1-2):
God is well-known and respected in Judah and Israel. He dwells in Jerusalem and Zion.

2. God's Victory Over Enemies (Verses 3-6):
God destroys weapons and defeats enemies, showing His unmatched power.

3. God's Majesty and Judgment (Verses 7-9):
No one can stand against God when He's angry. His judgment brings awe and silence.

4. God's Protection of the Humble (Verse 9):
God rises to judge and save the humble and oppressed.

5. Vow and Tribute to God (Verses 10-12):
We should make promises to God and keep them, bringing Him gifts. Even human anger can praise Him, and He humbles powerful rulers.

Psalm 77

Cry for Help and Remembrance

1. Cry for Help (Verses 1-3):
I cried out to God in my trouble, seeking His attention. In distress, I reached out to Him, refusing to find comfort.

2. Questions in Despair (Verses 4-9):
Feeling troubled, I wondered if God had abandoned us forever, if His promises failed, and if He forgot to be gracious.

3. Remembering God's Mighty Deeds (Verses 10-12):
Then I remembered the years when God showed His power, and I recalled His miracles of old.

4. God's Power and Holiness (Verses 13-15):
Your ways, O God, are holy. Who is as great as our God? You perform miracles and display Your power among the nations.

5. Recounting the Exodus (Verses 16-20):
You led Your people through the sea, guiding them like a shepherd leads his flock through the hands of Moses and Aaron.

Psalm 78
Teaching Through History

1. Purpose of the Psalm (Verses 1-4):
Listen, my people, to my teaching. I will speak of hidden things from the past, teaching lessons from long ago.

2. God's Deeds and Command to Remember (Verses 5-8):
God established His law and commanded our ancestors to teach their children, so they would know and follow Him.

3. Rebellion and God's Patience (Verses 9-39):
Despite God's miracles and provision, Israel rebelled in the wilderness, putting God to the test and sinning against Him repeatedly.

4. Miracles in Egypt and Provision in the Wilderness (Verses 40-55):
God performed wonders in Egypt, parting the sea and providing for His people in the wilderness.

5. Continued Rebellion and Consequences (Verses 56-64):
Despite God's care, the people rebelled, leading to military defeats and suffering.

6. God's Choice of Zion and David (Verses 65-72):
God chose David to shepherd His people from the sheep pens, establishing His reign on Mount Zion.

Psalm 79
Cry for Deliverance

1. Israel under persecution (v.1-7):

God, our enemies have invaded Your land, defiled Your temple, and left Jerusalem in ruins. They've treated Your servants' bodies as food for birds and beasts. Blood flows like water, and there's no one to bury the dead. We're mocked and scorned by our neighbors. How long, Lord, will You stay angry? They've devastated our homes and devoured our people.

2. Prayer for deliverance (v.8-13):

Please don't hold our past sins against us. Show us Your mercy quickly, for we are in great distress. Help us, God, for the glory of Your name. Save us and forgive our sins. Preserve those marked for death. We, Your people, will forever thank You and praise Your name.

PSALM 80
Asaph - Prayer for Israel's Restoration

1. Prayer of Israel (v.1-7):

Listen, Shepherd of Israel, who leads Joseph like a flock. Shine forth and save us. Turn us back to You, God, and make Your face shine upon us. How long will You be angry with our prayers? You've fed us tears and made us a laughingstock to our enemies. Turn us back to You, God, and make Your face shine upon us.

2. Prayer of the church, the vine (v.8-19):

You brought a vine out of Egypt, cleared the land, and planted it. It flourished, spreading its branches far and wide. But now its walls are broken, and it's being destroyed. Please, God, look down from heaven, visit this vine, and protect it. Strengthen the one You've chosen, and we won't turn away from You. Revive us, and we'll call on Your name. Turn us back to You, Lord God Almighty, and make Your face shine upon us, so we'll be saved.

PSALM 81

God's Redemption and Call to Obedience

1. God redeemed Israel from Egypt and gave His commandments (v.1-7):
Sing praises to God, our strength. Make joyful noises to the God of Jacob. Play music and instruments to celebrate our appointed times. These are statutes for Israel, reminders of God's deliverance. He freed us from burdens and answered us in times of trouble.

2. God called Israel but they went their own way (v.8-12):
Listen, my people, and I will testify to you. If only you would listen to me, your God who brought you out of Egypt. Open wide your mouth, and I will fill it. But you didn't listen; you followed your own desires, so I left you to your own devices.

3. God is ready to help and bless if we heed His words (v.13-16):
Oh, if only you had listened, I would have subdued your enemies and satisfied you with the finest wheat and honey from the rock.

Psalm 82

God's Judgment on the Wicked

1. God sees the wickedness of gentile gods (v.1-5):
God presides in the heavenly council and judges among the gods. How long will you defend the unjust and show favoritism to the wicked? They walk in darkness, ignorant of the foundations of the earth.

2. God says the gentile gods will perish like men (v.6,7):
Though called gods, they will die like men, falling like princes.

3. Only one God, Jehovah, is the true judge (v.8):
Rise up, O God, and judge the earth, for all nations belong to You.

PSALM 83
The Prayer Against Enemies

The wicked counsel of the enemies (v.3-5):
Enemies plot against God's people, aiming to erase Israel's name from memory. They conspire together, seeking Israel's destruction.

The enemy nations (v.6-8):
Various nations, including Edom, Ishmaelites, Moab, and Philistines, join forces against Israel.

Judgment to seek the Lord (v.16-18):
Prayer for shame upon the enemies, leading them to seek God's name. Let them be confused and perish, so all may know that Jehovah reigns supreme.

PSALM 84
The Blessing of Dwelling in God's House

Blessing of dwelling in the house of God (v.1-7):
Praise for the tabernacles of the Lord, where souls long to be. Blessed are those who dwell in God's house, continually praising Him. Even passing through difficult valleys becomes a source of refreshment, and strength grows in His presence.

Prayer and trust in God (v.8-12):
Prayer for God's attention and favor upon His anointed. Better is a day in God's courts than a thousand elsewhere. The Lord is a sun and shield, granting grace and glory to the upright. Blessed is the one who trusts in Him.

Psalm 85
Hopeful Prayer for Restoration

Hopeful prayer for the restoration of Israel (v.1-7):
Gratitude for God's favor and forgiveness, praying for revival and salvation. Confidence in God's mercy and salvation for His people.
Confidence in the prayer (v.8-13):
Assurance that God will speak peace to His people, if they turn from folly. Salvation is near those who fear Him. Mercy and truth, righteousness and peace, will prevail. The Lord will grant goodness and prosperity, guiding His people in righteousness.

PSALM 86
David's Prayer

Prayer (v.1-4):
David pleads for God's attention, acknowledging his own neediness and reliance on God's mercy. He lifts up his soul to God, seeking His favor and rejoicing in His salvation.

Praising God (v.5):
David praises God's goodness, forgiveness, and abundant mercy toward those who call upon Him.

Prayer (v.6-7):
He asks God to hear his prayer in times of trouble, expressing confidence that God will answer him.

Declaring there is no other God (v.8-10):
David declares God's uniqueness and greatness, acknowledging that all nations will worship and glorify Him.

Prayer (v.11-13):
David seeks God's guidance, pledging to walk in His truth and praising Him for His mercy and deliverance.

Fear from pride (v.14):
David expresses his fear of the proud and violent who seek his soul without regard for God.

Praising God (v.15):
Despite his troubles, David extols God's compassion, grace, patience, and abundant mercy.

Prayer ended in confidence (v.16-17):
David concludes by appealing for God's mercy, strength, and

salvation, asking for a sign of His favor to shame his enemies and affirming his trust in God's help and comfort.

PSALM 87
The Glory of the City of God

Declaration of the glorious city of God (v.1-3):
The psalmist celebrates the holy city of Zion, declaring its foundation in the holy mountains and God's love for its gates.

Those who enter in the kingdom age are registered as born again (v.4-7):
People from various nations are counted as born in Zion, and God will establish her. Singers and players of instruments will be there, and all blessings come from God.

PSALM 88

The Prayer of Hope in the Time of Sufferings

The prayer of hope in the time of sufferings (v.1-7):
The psalmist cries out to God day and night, overwhelmed by troubles and feeling near death. He feels abandoned by God, surrounded by darkness and affliction.

God locked him not to go out and all left him (v.8-18):
The psalmist feels isolated and abandoned, with no strength left. He laments being rejected by friends and loved ones, feeling as if God's wrath is upon him.

Psalm 89
Meditation of Ethan the Ezrahite

Praising God for His mercies of covenant (v.1-4):
Ethan praises God's everlasting mercies and faithfulness, especially in His covenant with David, promising to establish his throne forever.

God praised in heaven (v.5-8):
The heavens and the assembly of the saints praise God's wonders and His unmatched greatness and faithfulness.

All creatures praise God (v.9-12):
God's sovereignty over creation is celebrated, including His control over the sea and His victory over enemies.

David was chosen by God (v.13-29):
Ethan recounts God's choice of David, emphasizing His promise to strengthen and protect him, exalt his descendants, and maintain His covenant with him.

Warning of God for the descendants (v.29-32):
While God promises to uphold His covenant, He warns that disobedience will result in punishment for David's descendants.

Still God keeps His covenant (v.33-37):
Despite potential consequences for disobedience, God affirms His commitment to David's line and promises to maintain His covenant forever.

God punished according to His covenant (v.38-45):
Ethan laments God's apparent rejection of His covenant, as David's descendants suffer defeat and humiliation, questioning how long this punishment will last.

Prayer in the distress and punishment of God (v.46-52): Ethan pleads for God's intervention, reminding Him of His promises to David and the reproach suffered by His servants. He concludes with a blessing to the Lord forever.

PSALM 90
The Prayer of Moses

Man's dwelling place in God (v.1-2):
Moses acknowledges God as the eternal refuge of humanity, even before the creation of the earth and the world.

The temporality of human life (v.3-6):
Moses reflects on the brevity of human existence, likening it to grass that flourishes in the morning but withers by evening.

God's awareness of our sins (v.7-11):
He acknowledges God's perception of human iniquities and emphasizes the fleeting nature of life under God's wrath.

The importance of prayer and wisdom (v.12-17):
Moses prays for wisdom in recognizing the brevity of life, asking for God's compassion, mercy, and favor upon His servants.

PSALM 91
Dwelling in the Secret Place

Security in God's protection (v.1-2):
The psalmist affirms the security found in dwelling in God's secret place and declares trust in God as refuge and fortress.

God's daily protection (v.3-8):
Assurance is given of God's deliverance from various dangers, including diseases like the pestilence mentioned, and the promise that no harm will befall those who trust in Him.

Trusting in God's providence (v.9-10):
The psalmist reinforces the belief that those who make God their refuge will be shielded from evil and harm.

Angel's protection and divine favor (v.11-13):
God is depicted as sending His angels to protect those who trust in Him, ensuring their safety even in the face of dangerous creatures.

Promise of divine deliverance and salvation (v.14-16):
The psalmist speaks of the rewards for those who love and know God, including deliverance from trouble, honor, and the assurance of long life and salvation.

Psalm 92
A Song for the Sabbath Day

The Privilege of Worship (v.1-6):
The psalmist extols the goodness of giving thanks and singing praises to God's name, recognizing His lovingkindness and faithfulness. He rejoices in God's works and acknowledges His greatness.

Contrast Between the Wicked and the Righteous (v.7-15): While the wicked may seem to flourish temporarily, they will ultimately be destroyed. In contrast, the righteous will flourish like palm trees and cedars, planted in the house of the Lord, bearing fruit even in old age to declare God's righteousness.

PSALM 93
The Eternal Kingdom of God

God's Reign and Majesty (v.1-2):
The psalmist proclaims the Lord's sovereignty and majesty, emphasizing the stability and permanence of His kingdom.

God's Power Over Chaos (v.3-4):
Even in the face of tumultuous waters, the Lord's might surpasses them all, highlighting His supremacy over chaos and disorder.

God's Holiness and Faithfulness (v.5):
The psalm concludes by affirming the certainty of God's testimonies and the eternal holiness of His house.

PSALM 94
The Judgment Seat of Christ

Appeal for Divine Vengeance (v.1-3):
The psalmist calls upon God to rise up and render judgment upon the proud and wicked who oppress His people.

Exposure of the Wicked (v.4-7):
The wicked boast in their evil deeds, believing that God does not see or understand their actions. However, the psalmist reminds them that God knows all and will bring righteous judgment.

Assurance of God's Justice (v.8-11):
The psalmist contrasts the futility of the wicked with the blessedness of those whom God instructs and teaches. He affirms that judgment will return to righteousness.

Comfort in God's Help (v.12-19):
The psalmist finds solace in the Lord's assistance, acknowledging that without Him, he would falter. He trusts in God's mercy and finds comfort in His presence amidst anxieties.

Condemnation of Worldly Judgment (v.20-21):
The psalmist condemns the throne of iniquity that devises evil by law and condemns the innocent. He questions whether such judgment can have fellowship with God.

Hope for the Righteous (v.22-23):
The psalmist finds assurance in God as his defense and refuge. He trusts that God will bring justice upon the wicked and protect His

people.

Psalm 95
A Call to Worship

Invitation to Worship (v.1-7):

The psalmist calls upon all to sing joyfully to the Lord, the Rock of their salvation. They are urged to come before His presence with thanksgiving and praise, acknowledging His greatness as the Creator of all things.

Warning Against Hardened Hearts (v.8-11):

A solemn warning is given against hardening one's heart, as the Israelites did during the rebellion in the wilderness. Despite witnessing God's works, they tested Him and were consequently denied entry into His rest. This serves as a cautionary tale against disobedience and unbelief.

PSALM 96
A Song of Praise to God

Proclamation of God's Glory (v.1-3):
The psalmist exhorts all the earth to sing a new song to the Lord, proclaiming His salvation and declaring His glory among the nations. The greatness and splendor of God are emphasized above all other gods.

Call to Worship (v.4-9):
All are called to ascribe glory and strength to the Lord, offering Him the worship due His name. They are urged to tremble before Him and worship in the beauty of holiness, acknowledging His reign and righteous judgment.

Anticipation of God's Coming (v.10-13):
The heavens and earth are called to rejoice at the imminent coming of the Lord to judge the world with righteousness and truth. All creation is depicted as rejoicing before Him, anticipating His righteous rule.

PSALM 97
Praise to the Sovereign Lord

Declaration of God's Reign (v.1-6):
The psalmist announces the reign of the Lord and the righteousness and justice that underpin His throne. His presence is described as awe-inspiring, causing even the mountains to melt like wax.

Call to Worship (v.7-9):
All are called to worship the Lord and reject idols, acknowledging His supremacy over all the earth. The righteous are encouraged to rejoice in His preservation and deliverance.

Joy of the Righteous (v.10-12):
Those who love the Lord are urged to hate evil and rejoice in His righteousness. Light and gladness are promised to the upright in heart, who are called to give thanks and rejoice in the remembrance of His holy name.

PSALM 98
Praise to the Lord

Celebration of God's Marvelous Deeds (v.1-3):
The psalmist calls for a new song of praise to the Lord for His
marvelous deeds and victories. God's salvation and righteousness
are proclaimed to the nations, and His mercy to the house of
Israel is remembered. All the earth is summoned to shout joyfully,
sing praises, and play music in honor of the Lord, who is coming
to judge the earth with righteousness and equity.

Psalm 99

Praise to the Lord for His Holiness

Acknowledgment of God's Greatness (v.1-3):
The psalmist declares that the Lord reigns and is exalted above all peoples, dwelling between the cherubim. His name is praised as great and awesome, for He is holy.

Recognition of God's Righteousness (v.4,5):
It is acknowledged that the King's strength is accompanied by justice and equity. The Lord is praised and worshiped as holy.

Communion with His Saints (v.6-9):
The psalmist recalls the examples of Moses, Aaron, and Samuel, who called upon the Lord and received His answers. God communicated with them in the cloudy pillar, giving them His testimonies and ordinances. Despite His ability to forgive, He also takes vengeance on their deeds. Once again, the Lord is exalted and worshiped at His holy hill as the holy God.

PSALM 100
A Psalm of Thanksgiving

Call to Joyful Worship (v.1,2):
A joyful shout is called upon all the earth to praise the Lord with gladness and singing. It is proclaimed that the Lord is God, the Creator of all, and His people are the sheep of His pasture.

Entrance into His Presence (v.3,4):
All are urged to enter into the Lord's presence with thanksgiving and praise, acknowledging His goodness, everlasting mercy, and enduring truth.

Conclusion (v.5):
The psalm concludes with a reaffirmation of the Lord's goodness, mercy, and truth, which endure for all generations.

Psalm 101
Principles of Righteous Rule

Praise and Commitment (v.1-2):
David begins by expressing his intention to sing of mercy and justice and to praise the Lord. He declares his commitment to walk with integrity within his house and to lead with a perfect heart.

Commitment to Righteousness (v.3-5):
David vows to avoid wickedness and evil influences, refusing to entertain sinful behavior or those who practice it. He resolves to distance himself from those with perverse hearts and to destroy those who slander their neighbors or display pride and haughtiness.

Recognition and Reward for the Righteous (v.6-8):
David promises to honor and dwell with the faithful and those who walk in a perfect way. He pledges not to tolerate deceit or lies but to establish righteousness in his household and city.

Judgment against the Wicked (v.8-9):
David declares his intention to early destroy all the wicked and cut off evildoers from the city of the Lord, demonstrating his commitment to uphold justice and righteousness.

PSALM 102
The Lord's Eternal Love

Prayer of the Afflicted (v.1-11):
The psalmist, overwhelmed and afflicted, cries out to the Lord, pleading for His attention and mercy. He describes his suffering and distress, comparing himself to birds of the wilderness and expressing his anguish at the consequences of God's wrath.

Hope for Restoration (v.12-22):
Despite his suffering, the psalmist expresses hope in the enduring nature of the Lord. He anticipates God's favor on Zion and the rebuilding of the temple. He foresees a time when the nations will fear the Lord and serve Him, and when the oppressed will be released and praised.

Eternal Nature of God (v.23-28):
The psalmist reflects on the eternal nature of God, who laid the foundation of the earth and remains unchanged throughout all generations. He acknowledges that while everything else may perish, God endures forever. The psalmist finds comfort in the assurance that the descendants of God's servants will continue to be established before Him.

PSALM 103
David Praises for the Lord's Mercies

Worship for Redemption and Mercy (v.1-5):
David calls upon his soul and all within him to bless the Lord and not forget His benefits. He acknowledges God's forgiveness, healing, redemption from destruction, and crowning with lovingkindness and tender mercies. David praises God for satisfying him with good things and renewing his youth.

Explanation of God's Love (v.6-13):
David reflects on God's execution of righteousness and justice for the oppressed. He emphasizes God's mercy, graciousness, and slowness to anger, contrasting human transience with God's everlasting mercy. David describes God's forgiveness and compares His compassion to that of a father for his children.

Recognition of Human Frailty (v.14-16):
David acknowledges God's understanding of human nature, recognizing humanity's frailty and mortality. He compares human life to grass and flowers that wither and vanish swiftly.

Continued Worship in the Kingdom Age (v.17-22):
David affirms the everlasting nature of God's mercy and righteousness for those who fear Him and keep His covenant. He acknowledges God's established throne and kingdom and calls upon angels, hosts, and all creation to bless and worship the Lord.

PSALM 104
Praises His Creation and Providence

Majesty of God (v.1-4):
The psalmist begins by blessing the Lord and acknowledging His greatness, honor, and majesty. He describes God's clothing with light, the stretching out of the heavens, and His use of clouds and winds as chariots.

Creation of Earth (v.5-9):
The psalmist praises God for laying the foundations of the earth and covering it with waters. He describes God's control over the waters and their boundaries, preventing them from covering the earth again.

God's Provision for Creatures (v.10-18):
The psalmist marvels at God's provision of springs, grass, and vegetation for animals and birds. He highlights how God satisfies creatures' thirst and hunger and provides them with homes and habitats.

Purpose of Planets (v.19-24):
The psalmist reflects on God's appointment of the moon and sun for seasons and the cycle of day and night. He observes how animals rely on these rhythms for their activities while humans work during the day.

The Great Sea's Wealth (v.25-30):
The psalmist praises God's creation of the sea, filled with countless

living creatures. He describes ships sailing and Leviathan playing in the waters, all depending on God's provision. He recognizes God's control over life and death and His renewal of the earth.

Call to Praise and Worship (v.31-35):
The psalmist concludes by praying for God's glory to endure forever and rejoicing in His works. He expresses his commitment to sing and praise God and calls for the removal of sinners and wickedness. He blesses the Lord and urges others to praise Him.

Psalm 105
Eternal Faithfulness of the Lord

Thanksgiving and Praise (v.1-5):
The psalmist calls upon the people to give thanks to the Lord, sing praises to Him, and speak of His wondrous works. He encourages rejoicing in God's holy name and seeking His strength and presence continually. The psalmist reminds the descendants of Abraham and Jacob of God's covenant and everlasting faithfulness.

God's Covenant with Abraham (v.6-15):
The psalmist recounts God's covenant with Abraham, Isaac, and Jacob, promising them the land of Canaan. Despite their few numbers and status as strangers in the land, God protected them and rebuked kings for their sake, safeguarding His chosen people.

Joseph's Journey to Egypt (v.17-22):
The psalmist describes Joseph's trials, from being sold as a slave to becoming ruler over Egypt. Despite the hardships, God's plan prevailed, and Joseph ultimately rose to power, using his position to save his family.

Israel's Sojourn in Egypt (v.23-25):
The psalmist recounts how Jacob and his descendants came to dwell in Egypt, where they multiplied and grew stronger. However, the Egyptians turned against them, leading to their enslavement.

God's Deliverance through Moses (v.26-36):
The psalmist recalls how God sent Moses and Aaron to deliver Israel from Egypt. Through miraculous signs and wonders, including darkness, plagues, and the parting of the Red Sea, God liberated His people from bondage.

Israel's Exodus and Provision (v.37-45):
The psalmist describes Israel's departure from Egypt, emphasizing how they left with abundance and strength. God provided for them in the wilderness, guiding them with a cloud and fire, and sustaining them with food and water. He fulfilled His promise to Abraham by giving them the land of the Gentiles, enabling them to observe His statutes and laws. The psalm concludes with praise to the Lord for His faithfulness and provision.

PSALM 106
Remembrance of God's Salvation

Praise and Thanksgiving (v.1-5):
The psalm begins with a call to praise and give thanks to the Lord for His goodness and enduring mercy. It acknowledges the difficulty of fully expressing God's mighty acts and praises those who consistently practice justice and righteousness. The psalmist appeals to God for salvation and rejoices in the blessings of being among His chosen people.

Sins of Israel Despite God's Salvation (v.6-43):
The psalm recounts the repeated cycle of Israel's sinfulness and God's salvation throughout their history. Despite witnessing God's wonders and deliverance from Egypt, the Israelites rebelled against Him, forgetting His mercies and testing Him in the wilderness. They grumbled, worshipped idols, and disobeyed God's commands, provoking His anger. Yet, God repeatedly saved them for the sake of His name and His covenant with their forefathers, often in response to the intercession of righteous individuals like Moses and Phinehas.

God's Grace Despite Israel's Failures (v.44-48):
Despite Israel's persistent disobedience and rebellion, God showed compassion and remembered His covenant when they cried out to Him in affliction. He heard their pleas, relented from His anger, and showed mercy, even causing their captors to pity them. The

psalm concludes with a prayer for God to gather His people from among the nations, to save them, and to enable them to give thanks and praise to His holy name.

This psalms is a reminder of humanity's tendency to forget God's faithfulness and goodness, often succumbing to sin despite experiencing His salvation. Yet, it also highlights God's enduring mercy and grace, even in the face of repeated disobedience. It encourages repentance, reliance on God's mercy, and gratitude for His continual deliverance.

Psalm 107
Thanksgiving for His Great Works

Call to Thanksgiving (v.1-3):
The psalm begins with an exhortation to give thanks to the Lord for His enduring mercy and redemption. It emphasizes that those whom God has redeemed from various lands should openly declare His goodness and deliverance.

Guidance in the Wilderness (v.4-9):
God's provision and guidance in the wilderness are highlighted, emphasizing His satisfaction of the hungry soul and the longing soul with goodness. This section underscores God's care for His people even in barren and desolate places.

Deliverance from Captivity (v.10-16):
The psalm recounts how disobedience led to captivity, but in their distress, the people cried out to God, and He delivered them from their affliction. Once again, thanksgiving is demanded for God's mercy and salvation.

Healing from Affliction (v.17-22):
Despite further transgressions leading to affliction and sickness, God showed compassion by healing them. This section emphasizes the power of God's word to heal and deliver from destruction, prompting another call for thanksgiving.

Deliverance from the Sea (v.23-32):
God's sovereignty over the sea and His ability to calm storms

are celebrated. Those who travel and work at sea witness His miraculous intervention, leading them to praise and thanksgiving for His guidance and protection.

Conclusion: Call to Praise (v.33-43):
The psalm concludes by calling on all who are wise to observe and understand the lovingkindness of the Lord manifested in His righteous judgments. It emphasizes the importance of giving thanks to God for His wonderful works among humanity.

PSALM 108

David's Assurance of God's Victory

Glorifying God (v.1-6):
David expresses his steadfastness and determination to praise God with music and song. He acknowledges God's greatness and mercy, exalting Him above all the earth and seeking deliverance for His beloved.

The Promise of God (v.7-9):
David recalls God's promises and declares His victory over various nations, symbolized by the territories He claims as His own. This section emphasizes God's sovereignty and ultimate triumph.

Prayer and Hope (v.10-13):
David prays for God's help and acknowledges the futility of relying on human aid. He expresses confidence in God's power to grant victory over enemies, reaffirming trust in His divine intervention.

PSALM 109
David's Plea in the Face of False Accusations

When the Righteous Face False Accusations (v.1-5):
David begins by pleading with God not to remain silent in the face of the wicked who have slandered him with lies, surrounded him with hatred, and fought against him unjustly. Despite his love towards them, they have rewarded him with evil.

Prayer for Judgment on Accusers (v.6-20):
David calls upon God to let the accusations brought against him be met with divine judgment. He describes the depth of his suffering and the injustice he has faced. Yet, he maintains hope in God's mercy and prays for deliverance from his adversaries.

Hope in Suffering (v.21-31):
In his distress, David appeals to God's mercy, acknowledging his own weakness and neediness. He expresses confidence that God will save him, vindicate him, and bring shame upon his accusers. David resolves to praise the Lord wholeheartedly, trusting in His intervention to save the oppressed.

Psalm 110
The Eternal Priesthood of Christ

Fivefold Description of Christ (v.1, 2, 4, 6):
This psalms provides a prophetic description of Christ, portraying Him as God, King, Priest, Judge, and Mighty Warrior. This psalm foreshadows Jesus Christ's eternal priesthood and His reign over all creation.

Twofold Description of Christ's People (v.3, 7):
In addition to describing Christ, this psalm also speaks of His people, portraying them as both priests and soldiers. This reflects the New Testament teaching that believers are both priests who intercede for others and soldiers engaged in spiritual warfare against evil.

PSALM 111
Praise to God for His Mighty Works

Praise and Thanksgiving (v.1-3):
The psalmist begins with a declaration of praise to the Lord, vowing to praise Him wholeheartedly among the upright and in the congregation. He acknowledges the greatness and honor of God's works, expressing delight in studying them.

Graciousness of God (v.4-6):
God's graciousness and compassion towards His people are highlighted, as well as His provision for those who fear Him and His faithfulness to His covenant. The psalmist praises God for revealing the power of His works and granting His people the inheritance of nations.

Faithfulness and Salvation (v.7-9):
The psalmist extols the faithfulness and righteousness of God's precepts, affirming their enduring nature and truth. He acknowledges God's role as Savior, sending redemption to His people and establishing His covenant forever, declaring the holiness and awesomeness of His name.

Fear of the Lord and Wisdom (v.10-11):
The psalm concludes by asserting that the fear of the Lord is the beginning of wisdom, leading to a good understanding of His commandments. The psalmist affirms the enduring nature of God's praise.

PSALM 112
Blessings of the Righteous

Characteristics of the Righteous (v.1-3, 5, 9):
The righteous fear the Lord, delight in His commandments, are gracious, full of compassion, and deal graciously and lend. Their hearts are steadfast, trusting in the Lord.

Blessings Promised (v.1-3, 6-9):

- Wealth and riches will be in their house.
- Their righteousness endures forever.
- Light arises in the darkness for them.
- They will never be shaken.
- They will be in everlasting remembrance.
- They will not be afraid of evil tidings.
- Their horn will be exalted with honor.

PSALM 113

Praise for the Majesty and Grace of God

Majesty of God (v.1-5):

- The psalmist calls upon the servants of the Lord to praise His name forever.
- The Lord's name is exalted above all nations and His glory above the heavens.
- There is none like the Lord, who dwells on high.

Grace to the Needy (v.6-9):

- Despite His majesty, God humbles Himself to behold the heavens and the earth.
- He raises the poor from the dust and lifts the needy from the ash heap, seating them with princes.
- He grants the barren woman a home, blessing her with children.

PSALM 114

God's Redemption and Earth's Response

God's Redemption of Israel (v.1-8):

- The psalm recounts how Israel left Egypt, and the house of Jacob became God's sanctuary.
- The sea, Jordan, mountains, and little hills responded to God's presence with awe and obedience.

PSALM 115
Glory to God Alone

Glory to God Alone (v.1-3):

- The psalmist acknowledges that glory belongs to God alone, attributing it to His mercy and truth.
- God is sovereign in heaven, doing as He pleases.

Futility of Idols (v.4-8):

- Idols made by human hands are futile, possessing no senses or abilities.
- Those who make and trust in idols become like them, devoid of true understanding.

Trust in the Lord for Blessing (v.9-15):

- Israel and those who fear the Lord are encouraged to trust in Him, as He is their help and shield.
- The Lord remembers and blesses His people, both small and great.

Earth Given to Glorify God (v.16-18):

- While the heavens belong to the Lord, He has given the earth to humanity.

- The psalmist resolves to bless the Lord forever, acknowledging His sovereignty and worthiness of praise.

PSALM 116
Thanksgiving for Deliverance

Thanksgiving for Deliverance from Death (v.1-7):

- The psalmist expresses love for the Lord because He heard his supplications and delivered him from the pains of death.
- Despite trouble and sorrow, the psalmist called upon the name of the Lord, who saved him.
- The Lord's graciousness and righteousness are acknowledged, along with His mercy towards the simple.

Thanksgiving for Redemption of Soul (v.8-14):

- The psalmist praises God for delivering his soul from death, tears, and falling.
- In response, the psalmist vows to walk before the Lord in the land of the living, acknowledging his belief, affliction, and haste in calling upon the Lord.
- Gratitude is expressed through taking up the cup of salvation, paying vows to the Lord, and praising Him in the presence of all His people.

Death is Precious (v.15):

The psalmist reflects on the preciousness of death in the sight of the Lord, particularly the death of His saints.

Thanksgiving for Redemption of Slavery (v.16-19):

- Acknowledging servanthood to the Lord, the psalmist offers a sacrifice of thanksgiving and vows to call upon the name of the Lord.
- Vows are to be paid in the presence of all God's people, in the courts of the Lord's house, and in Jerusalem.

PSALM 117
Praise for God's Great Merciful Kindness

Praise for God's Merciful Kindness (v.1-2):

The psalm calls upon all nations and peoples to praise the Lord for His great merciful kindness, emphasizing the enduring truth of the Lord.

PSALM 118
Praise for God's Everlasting Mercy

Praise for God's Everlasting Mercy (v.1-4):

Thanksgiving is offered to the Lord for His enduring mercy, with Israel, the house of Aaron, and all who fear the Lord joining in praise.

Trust in the Lord (v.5-9):

The psalmist recounts calling upon the Lord in distress and experiencing His deliverance, affirming that it is better to trust in the Lord than in humans or princes.

Victory over Enemies (v.10-15):

- Despite being surrounded by nations, the psalmist trusts in the name of the Lord for victory over enemies, likening them to bees and a fire of thorns.
- The Lord is praised as the source of strength, song, and salvation.

Entrance to the Gate of Righteousness (v.19-21):

- The psalmist seeks entry to the gates of righteousness to praise the Lord, acknowledging them as the gates through which the righteous shall enter.
- Praise is offered for the Lord's answer and salvation.

Jesus Christ, the Cornerstone (v.22-29):

- The rejected stone has become the chief cornerstone, a marvel in the eyes of the Lord.
- The psalmist rejoices in the day the Lord has made, seeking prosperity and blessing for the one who comes in the name of the Lord.
- God is praised as the giver of light and salvation, and the psalm concludes with gratitude for His enduring mercy.

PSALM 119

The Exaltation of God's Word

As the longest chapter in the Bible, Psalm 119 stands as a monumental declaration of the greatness and importance of God's Word. Organized into 22 stanzas, each representing a letter of the Hebrew alphabet, this psalm explores various facets of God's word, including its commandments, statutes, testimonies, law, precepts, word, and judgments.

1. The Commandments: Acknowledging God's commandments as the path to righteousness, the psalmist expresses a fervent desire to obey and meditate upon them.

2. The Statutes: Reflecting on God's statutes, the psalmist finds joy in obedience and seeks understanding and guidance in them.

3. The Testimonies: The psalmist rejoices in the testimonies of God, finding them to be a source of delight and wisdom, guiding his actions and thoughts.

4. The Law: Praising the law of the Lord, the psalmist recognizes its righteousness and its role in shaping his life and worldview.

5. The Precepts: Embracing God's precepts, the psalmist commits to diligent obedience, seeking to walk in the ways of righteousness.

6. The Word: Treasuring the Word of God, the psalmist finds it to be a source of guidance, comfort, and strength, illuminating his

path and enriching his soul.

7. The Judgments: Revering God's judgments, the psalmist acknowledges their righteousness and prays for understanding and deliverance in accordance with them.

Blessings of the Word of God:

- Experience the transformative power of the Word, which cleanses, revives, strengthens, and establishes.
- Find protection, comfort, guidance, and assurance in the Word, which illuminates, upholds, and brings peace and salvation.

Psalm 120
Prayer for Deliverance from Enemies

- As pilgrims ascend to Jerusalem's sacred feasts,
- In my anguish, I cried out to the Lord, and He listened.
- Rescue my soul, O Lord, from deceitful tongues and lying lips.
- What punishment awaits you, O false tongue?
- Arrows honed by warriors and coals from the broom tree!
- Woe to me, for I dwell among those of Meshech and Kedar,
- Who harbor enmity instead of peace.

- I am a proponent of peace, yet they crave conflict when I speak.

Psalm 121

The Lord the Keeper of Israel

- The Lord is our protector.
- I lift my eyes to the hills—where does my help come from?
- My help comes from the Lord, Creator of heaven and earth.
- He will not let your foot slip; He who watches over you will not slumber.
- Behold, He who watches over Israel neither slumbers nor sleeps.
- The Lord is your protector; He is your shade at your right hand.
- The sun will not harm you by day, nor the moon by night.
- The Lord will keep you safe from all harm; He will watch over your life.

- The Lord will watch over your coming and going both now and forevermore.

Psalm 122

The Joy of Going to the House of the Lord

- The Lord is our unity.
- I rejoiced when they said to me, "Let us go to the house of the Lord."
- Our feet stand within your gates, O Jerusalem!
- Jerusalem, compact and unified, where the tribes gather,
- To seek the counsel of the Lord and give thanks to His name.
- For there sit the thrones of judgment, the thrones of the house of David.
- Pray for the peace of Jerusalem: May those who love her prosper.
- May peace reign within your walls and prosperity within your palaces.
- For the sake of my kin and companions, I pray for peace within you.

- For the sake of the house of the Lord our God, I seek your well-being.

PSALM 123
Prayer for Mercy

- The Lord is our source of mercy.
- To You, I lift my eyes, O dweller of the heavens.
- Just as servants look to their masters and maids to their mistresses,
- So we look to the Lord our God until He shows us mercy.
- Have mercy on us, O Lord, have mercy! For we endure great contempt.

- Our souls are filled with scorn from those at ease, with disdain from the proud.

PSALM 124
The Lord the Defense of His People

- The Lord is our refuge.
- "If the Lord had not been on our side," let Israel declare,
- "If the Lord had not been on our side when men rose up against us,
- They would have swallowed us alive when their anger flared against us;
- The torrents would have engulfed us; the raging waters would have swept over our souls;
- The floods would have overwhelmed us, sweeping over our lives."
- Blessed be the Lord, who did not leave us to be torn apart by their teeth.
- Our souls have escaped like a bird from the fowler's snare; the trap has been broken, and we are free.

- Our help is in the name of the Lord, the Maker of heaven and earth.

Psalm 125
The Lord Surrounds His People

- The Lord is our source of strength.
- Those who rely on the Lord are like Mount Zion, which cannot be shaken but endures forever.
- Just as the mountains surround Jerusalem, so the Lord surrounds His people, both now and forevermore.
- For the scepter of the wicked will not rest on the land allotted to the righteous, lest the righteous themselves turn to evil.
- O Lord, show kindness to those who are good and to those whose hearts are upright.

- But for those who stray into crooked paths, the Lord will lead them away with evildoers. Peace be upon Israel!

Psalm 126
A Joyful Return to Zion

- The Lord is our delight.
- When the Lord restored the fortunes of Zion, it seemed like a dream to us.
- Our mouths overflowed with laughter, and our tongues with joyful songs.
- The nations declared, "The Lord has done great things for them."
- Indeed, the Lord has done great things for us, and we are filled with joy.
- Restore our fortunes, O Lord, like streams in the Negev.
- Those who sow with tears will reap with songs of joy.

- Those who go out weeping, carrying seed to sow, will return with songs of joy, carrying sheaves with them.

PSALM 127
The Blessing of the Lord by Solomon

1. Dependence on the Lord for Success: Recognize that all labor and prosperity come from the Lord, as Jesus promised to build His church (Matthew 16:18).

2. Building and Protection: Acknowledge that success in personal and family life is futile without the Lord's intervention, for He alone can build and protect (1 Corinthians 3:11; Psalm 127:1).

3. Divine Provision: Understand that God provides food and rest to His beloved, relieving them from toil and worry (Matthew 6:25-34; Psalm 127:2).

4. Blessing of Children: Embrace children as a gift from the Lord, entrusted to parents for training in righteousness and as a source of joy and blessing (Psalm 127:3-4; Proverbs 22:6).

5. Legacy of Honor: Anticipate the honor and blessing that comes from having a fruitful family, which stands as a testament to God's faithfulness and provision (Psalm 127:5).

PSALM 128

Blessings for Those Who Fear the Lord

1. The Fear of the Lord: Discover abundant blessings in revering and walking in obedience to the Lord's ways (Psalm 128:1; Proverbs 9:10).

2. Fruitful Labor: Experience the satisfaction of enjoying the fruits of your labor, as advocated by the Apostle Paul (2 Thessalonians 3:7-13; Psalm 128:2).

3. Blessed Family Life: Cherish a wife who embodies strength and vitality within the home, reflecting the biblical ideal of a godly woman (Titus 2:3-5; Psalm 128:3).

4. Joyful Parenting: Delight in the presence of children who bring vitality and joy to the household, likened to flourishing olive plants around the table (Psalm 128:3; Psalm 127:3).

5. Heavenly Blessings: Receive abundant blessings from the heavenly Zion, symbolizing the outpouring of divine favor and provision (Psalm 128:5).

6. Community of Faith: Experience the goodness and unity within the community of believers, represented by the joys of Jerusalem (Psalm 128:5).

7. Generational Legacy: Witness the fulfillment of God's promises through the prosperity and faithfulness of future generations, a testament to His enduring faithfulness (Psalm 128:6).

8. Peaceful Abode: May the peace of God reign over your household, extending blessings and harmony to all aspects of life (Psalm 128:6).

PSALM 129

Persecution by the Wicked

- The Lord is our righteousness.
- From my youth, they have afflicted me, let Israel declare;
- From my youth, they have oppressed me, yet they have not prevailed against me.
- They have plowed my back with their furrows; they have made their marks long.

- But the Lord is righteous; He has cut the cords of the wicked.

PSALM 130
Waiting for the Redemption of the Lord

1. The Lord as Redeemer: Acknowledge the Lord as our redeemer, who lifts us from the depths of despair (v.1).
2. A Cry of Prayer: Pour out your soul to the Lord, crying out from the depths of your being, seeking His attentive ear (v.1,2).
3. Confidence in Forgiveness: Take solace in the forgiveness of sins, knowing that God's mercy exceeds His judgment (v.3,4).
4. Patient Waiting: Wait patiently for the Lord, placing your hope and trust in His promises, even in the darkest times (v.5,6).
5. Hope in God: Anchor your hope in the Lord, for in His mercy and abundant redemption, there is restoration and deliverance from all iniquities (v.7,8).

PSALM 131
Simple Trust in the Lord by David

The Lord is our hope.

1. Humble Submission: My heart is not proud, O Lord, nor are my eyes haughty. I do not concern myself with matters too great or lofty for me.
2. Tranquil Rest: Instead, I have calmed and quieted my soul, like a weaned child with its mother. My soul is like a weaned child within me.
3. Hope in the Lord: O Israel, put your hope in the Lord both now and forevermore.

PSALM 132
The Lord's Faithfulness to David

The Lord is our eternal dwelling place.

1. David's Desire to Build a Temple: David resolved to build a house for the Lord, swearing an oath to the Mighty One of Jacob, promising not to rest until he found a dwelling place for God (v.1-5).
2. Desire for God's Presence: Let us go to the Lord's tabernacle; let us worship at His footstool. Arise, O Lord, and come to Your resting place, You and the ark of Your strength (v.6-8).
3. God's Covenant with David: For the sake of David, the Lord made a covenant, promising to establish David's descendants on the throne if they remained faithful (v.9-12).
4. God's Choice of Zion: The Lord has chosen Zion as His dwelling place forever, promising to abundantly bless it and establish the reign of David's descendants (v.13-18).

Psalm 133
A Song of Unity

- How beautiful and pleasant it is when brothers and sisters live together in harmony!
- It's like the finest oil poured on the head, running down on the beard, flowing down Aaron's beard, onto the collar of his robe.

- It's like the dew of Mount Hermon falling on the hills of Zion. For there the Lord bestows his blessing, even life forevermore.

PSALM 134
A Song of Blessing

- Come, bless the Lord, all you who serve him, you who stand in the house of the Lord through the watches of the night.
- Lift up your hands in the sanctuary and praise the Lord.

- May the Lord, who made heaven and earth, bless you from Zion.

Psalm 135

His Mighty Deeds and Sovereign Power

- Praise the Lord! Praise the name of the Lord; praise him, you servants of the Lord, you who serve in the house of the Lord, in the courts of the house of our God.
- Praise the Lord, for the Lord is good; sing praises to his name, for that is pleasant.
- The Lord has chosen Jacob for himself, Israel as his treasured possession.

- I know that the Lord is great, that our Lord is greater than all gods.

- The Lord does whatever pleases him, in the heavens and on the earth, in the seas and all their depths.
- He makes clouds rise from the ends of the earth; he sends lightning with the rain and brings out the wind from his storehouses.
- He struck down the firstborn of Egypt, the firstborn of people and animals.

- He sent his signs and wonders into your midst, Egypt, against Pharaoh and all his servants.

- He struck down many nations and killed mighty kings—Sihon king of the Amorites, Og king of Bashan, and all the kings of Canaan—and he gave their land as an inheritance, an inheritance to his people Israel.

- Your name, Lord, endures forever, your renown, Lord, through all generations.

- For the Lord will vindicate his people and have compassion on his servants.

- The idols of the nations are silver and gold, made by human hands.
- They have mouths, but cannot speak, eyes, but cannot see.
- They have ears, but cannot hear, nor is there breath in their mouths.

- Those who make them will be like them, and so will all who trust in them.

- House of Israel, praise the Lord; house of Aaron, praise the Lord; house of Levi, praise the Lord; you who fear him, praise the Lord.

- Praise be to the Lord from Zion, to him who dwells in Jerusalem. Praise the Lord!

PSALM 136
A Song of God's Enduring Mercy

- Give thanks to the Lord, for he is good. His love endures forever.
- Give thanks to the God of gods. His love endures forever.
- Give thanks to the Lord of lords: His love endures forever.
- to him who alone does great wonders, His love endures forever.
- who by his understanding made the heavens, His love endures forever.

- who spread out the earth upon the waters, His love endures forever.
- who made the great lights— His love endures forever.
- the sun to govern the day, His love endures forever.
- the moon and stars to govern the night; His love endures forever.
- to him who struck down the firstborn of Egypt His love endures forever.
- and brought Israel out from among them His love endures forever.
- with a mighty hand and outstretched arm; His love endures forever.

- to him who divided the Red Sea asunder His love endures forever.
- and brought Israel through the midst of it, His love endures forever.
- but swept Pharaoh and his army into the Red Sea; His love endures forever.
- to him who led his people through the wilderness; His love endures forever.
- to him who struck down great kings; His love endures forever.
- and killed mighty kings— His love endures forever.
- Sihon king of the Amorites His love endures forever.
- and Og king of Bashan, His love endures forever.
- and gave their land as an inheritance, His love endures forever.
- an inheritance to his servant Israel. His love endures forever.
- He remembered us in our low estate. His love endures forever.
- and freed us from our enemies. His love endures forever.
- He gives food to every creature. His love endures forever.
- Give thanks to the God of heaven. His love endures forever.

PSALM 137
Remembering Zion in Exile

- By the rivers of Babylon we sat and wept when we remembered Zion.
- There on the poplars we hung our harps,
- for there our captors asked us for songs, our tormentors demanded songs of joy; they said, "Sing us one of the songs of Zion!"
- How can we sing the songs of the Lord while in a foreign land?
- If I forget you, Jerusalem, may my right hand forget its skill.
- May my tongue cling to the roof of my mouth if I do not remember you, if I do not consider Jerusalem my highest joy.
- Remember, Lord, what the Edomites did on the day Jerusalem fell. "Tear it down," they cried, "tear it down to its foundations!"
- Daughter Babylon, doomed to destruction, happy is the one who repays you according to what you have done to us.
- Happy is the one who seizes your infants and dashes them against the rocks.

Psalm 138

Thanksgiving for the Lord's Favor

1. Thanksgiving: I will praise you with all my heart; I'll sing your praises even in front of other gods.
2. Worship: I'll worship toward your holy temple and praise your name for your kindness and truth. You've honored your word above everything else.
3. Answered Prayer: When I called out to you, you answered me and gave me strength.
4. Praise from Kings: All the kings of the earth will praise you when they hear your words.
5. Confidence: Though you're high above, you care for the humble. Even in trouble, you'll revive me and save me.
6. Completion: You'll finish what you started in me. Your love lasts forever; don't abandon your work.

PSALM 139

The All-Knowing, Ever-Present God

1. God's Knowledge: You know everything about me, when I sit or stand, my thoughts, habits, words, and steps.
2. God's Wisdom: You wonderfully made me, even before I was born. Your thoughts about me are precious.
3. God's Presence: Even if I go to the highest heavens or the deepest depths, you're there. Even darkness can't hide me from you.
4. God's Care: Your care for me is beyond measure, always watching over me.

PSALM 140
Prayer for Protection from the Wicked

Prayer for Deliverance from Evil Men.
The poison of wicked men (v.1-3).

- Deliver me, O Lord, from evil men; Preserve me from violent men, who plan evil things in their hearts; They continually gather together for war.
- They sharpen their tongues like a serpent; The poison of asps is under their lips.

The snare of the wicked proud (v.4,5).

- Keep me, O Lord, from the hands of the wicked; Preserve me from violent men, who have purposed to make my steps stumble.
- The proud have hidden a snare for me, and cords; They have spread a net by the wayside; They have set traps for me.

The Prayer of a righteous (v.6-8).

- I said to the Lord: You are my God; Hear the voice of my supplications, O Lord.

- God the Lord, the strength of my salvation, You have covered my head on the day of battle.
- Do not grant, O Lord, the desires of the wicked; Do not further his wicked scheme, lest they be exalted.

The judgment on wicked men (v.9-11).

- As for the heads of those who surround me, Let the evil of their lips cover them; Let burning coals fall upon them; Let them be cast into the fire, into deep pits, that they rise not up again.
- Let not a slanderer be established in the earth; Let evil hunt the violent man to overthrow him.

The surety of upright (v.12,13).

- I know that the Lord will maintain The cause of the afflicted, And justice for the poor.
- Surely the righteous shall give thanks to Your name; The upright shall dwell in Your presence.

PSALM 141
Prayer for Safekeeping from Wickedness

Prayer of the righteous.

- Lord, I cry out to You; Make haste to me! Give ear to my voice when I cry out to You.
- Let my prayer be set before You as incense, The lifting up of my hands as the evening sacrifice.

Not to compromise the wicked talks (v.3,4).

- Set a guard, O Lord, over my mouth; Keep watch over the door of my lips.
- Do not incline my heart to any evil thing, to practice wicked works with men who work iniquity; And do not let me eat of their delicacies.

But to hear the words of a righteous (v.5).

Let the righteous strike me; It shall be a kindness. And let him rebuke me; It shall be excellent oil; Let my head not refuse it.
For still my prayer is against the deeds of the wicked (v.6-10).

- Their judges are overthrown by the sides of the cliff, and they hear my words, for they are sweet.
- Our bones are scattered at the mouth of the grave, as when one plows and breaks up the earth.
- But my eyes are upon You, O God the Lord; In You I take refuge; Do not leave my soul destitute.
- Keep me from the snares they have laid for me, And from the traps of the workers of iniquity.
- Let the wicked fall into their own nets, While I escape safely.

PSALM 142
A Cry for Help in Trouble

A Prayer when he was in the cave.

1. I cry out to the Lord with my voice; With my voice to the Lord I make my supplication.
2. I pour out my complaint before Him; I declare before Him my trouble.
3. When my spirit was overwhelmed within me, Then You knew my path.
4. In the way in which I walk They have secretly set a snare for me.
5. Look on my right hand and see, for there is no one who acknowledges me; Refuge has failed me; No one cares for my soul.
6. I cried out to You, O Lord: I said, You are my refuge, My portion in the land of the living.
7. Attend to my cry, For I am brought very low; Deliver me from my persecutors, for they are stronger than I.
8. Bring my soul out of prison, That I may praise Your name; The righteous shall surround me, For You shall deal bountifully with me.

PSALM 143
A Prayer for Deliverance and Guidance

Hear my prayer, O Lord, Give ear to my supplications! In Your faithfulness answer me, And in Your righteousness.

Do not enter into judgment with Your servant, for in Your sight no one living is righteous.

For the enemy has persecuted my soul; He has crushed my life to the ground; He has made me dwell in darkness, like those who have long been dead.

Therefore, my spirit is overwhelmed within me; My heart within me is distressed.

1. **I remember the days of old**; I meditate on all Your works; I muse on the work of Your hands. I spread out my hands to You; My soul longs for You like a thirsty land. Selah

2. **Answer me speedily**, O Lord; My spirit fails! Do not hide Your face from me, Lest I be like those who go down into the pit.

3. **Cause me to hear** Your lovingkindness in the morning, for in You do I trust; Cause me to know the way in which I should walk, For

I lift up my soul to You.

4. **Deliver me,** O Lord, from my enemies; In You I take shelter.
5. **Teach me** to do Your will, For You are my God; Your Spirit is good. Lead me in the land of uprightness.
6. **Revive me**, O Lord, for Your name's sake! For Your righteousness' sake bring my soul out of trouble.

In Your mercy cut off my enemies, and destroy all those who afflict my soul; For I am Your servant.

PSALM 144
A Prayer for Rescue and Prosperity

Happy are the people whose God is the Lord!

Blessed be the Lord my Rock, who trains my hands for war, and my fingers for battle—My lovingkindness and my fortress, my high tower and my deliverer, my shield and the One in whom I take refuge, who subdues my people under me.

What is man? (v.3,4).

Lord, what is man, that You take knowledge of him? Or the son of man, that You are mindful of him? Man is like a breath; His days are like a passing shadow.

Prayer to destroy the wicked (v.5-8).

Bow down Your heavens, O Lord, and come down; Touch the mountains, and they shall smoke. Flash forth lightning and scatter them; Shoot out Your arrows and destroy them. Their mouth speaks lying words, and whose right hand is a right hand of falsehood.

Prayer and praise for the salvation of God (v.9-15).

I will sing a new song to You, O God; On a harp of ten strings I will sing praises to You, The One who gives salvation to kings, who delivers David His Servant from the deadly sword.

Rescue me and deliver me from the hand of foreigners, whose mouth speaks lying words, and whose right hand is a right hand of falsehood—That our sons may be as plants grown up in their youth; That our daughters may be as pillars, Sculptured in palace style; That our barns may be full, supplying all kinds of produce; That our sheep may bring forth thousands and ten thousand in our fields; That our oxen may be well laden; That there be no breaking in or going out; That there be no outcry in our streets. Happy are the people who are in such a state; Happy are the people whose God is the Lord!

PSALM 145
A Song of God's Majesty and Love

The attributes of God, emphasizing His greatness, grace, and goodness.

1. God's Greatness: Reflect on the unsearchable greatness of God's works for us (v.3).
2. God's Grace: Acknowledge His graciousness, compassion, and mercy (v.8).
3. God's Goodness: Celebrate His goodness and provision for His creation (v.15).
4. God's Upholding: Trust in His steadfastness to uphold and support us (v.14).
5. God's Righteousness: Honor His righteousness in all His ways (v.17).
6. God's Listening Ear: Take comfort in the assurance that He hears our cries (v.18).
7. God's Preservation: Recognize His role in preserving all who love Him (v.20).
8. God's Majesty: Marvel at His glorious and everlasting kingdom (v.11).
9. God's Holiness: Reverence His holy name and nature (v.21).

10. God's Nearness: Experience His closeness to those who call upon Him in truth (v.18).
11. God's Response: Trust in His promise to hear our cry and save us (v.19).
12. God's Satisfaction: Find fulfillment in Him, as He satisfies the desires of those who fear Him (v.16, 19).

PSALM 146

The Happiness in the Lord

Praise the Lord! Praise the Lord, O my soul! While I live I will praise the Lord; I will sing praises to my God while I have my being.

Do not put trust in princes or a son of man, in whom there is no help (v.3,4).

His spirit departs, he returns to his earth; On that very day his plans perish.

Happy is he who has his help and hope in the Lord(v.5-7).

He made heaven and earth, the sea, and all that is in them; Who keeps truth forever, who executes justice for the oppressed, who gives food to the hungry.

The Lord gives freedom (v.8-10).

The Lord opens the eyes of the blind; The Lord raises those who are bowed down; The Lord loves the righteous. The Lord watches over the strangers; He relieves the fatherless and widow; But the way of the wicked He turns upside down.

The Lord shall reign forever (v.10).

Your God, O Zion, to all generations. Praise the Lord!

PSALM 147
Praise for His Word and Providence

Praise the Lord! For it is good to sing praises to our God; For it is pleasant, and praise is beautiful. Why? (v.1-6).

- The Lord builds up Jerusalem; He gathers together the outcasts of Israel.
- He heals the brokenhearted and binds up their wounds.
- He counts the number of the stars; He calls them all by name.
- Great is our Lord, and mighty in power; His understanding is infinite.
- The Lord lifts up the humble; He casts the wicked down to the ground.

Sing to the Lord with thanksgiving; Sing praises on the harp to our God. Why? (v.7-11).

- He covers the heavens with clouds,
- He prepares rain for the earth,
- He makes grass to grow on the mountains.
- He gives to the beast its food, and to the young ravens that cry.

- The Lord takes pleasure in those who fear Him, in those who hope in His mercy.

Praise the Lord, O Jerusalem! Praise your God, O Zion! Why? (v.12-20).

- He has strengthened the bars of your gates; He has blessed your children within you.
- He makes peace in your borders, and fills you with the finest wheat.
- He sends out His command to the earth; His word runs very swiftly.
- He gives snow like wool; He scatters the frost like ashes; He casts out His hail like morsels; Who can stand before His cold? He sends out His word and melts them; He causes His wind to blow, and the waters flow.
- He declares His word to Jacob, His statutes and His judgments to Israel.
- He has not dealt thus with any nation; And as for His judgments, they have not known them. Praise the Lord!

PSALM 148

All creatures worship the Lord

1. Praise the Lord! Praise the Lord from the heavens; Praise Him in the heights!
2. Praise Him, all His angels; Praise Him, all His hosts!
3. Praise Him, sun and moon; Praise Him, all you stars of light!
4. Praise Him, you heavens of heavens, and you water above the heavens!
5. Let them praise the name of the Lord, For He commanded and they were created.
6. He also established them forever and ever; He made a decree which shall not pass away.
7. Praise the Lord from the earth, you great sea creatures and all the depths; Fire and hail, snow and clouds; Stormy wind, fulfilling His word; Mountains and all hills; Fruitful trees and all cedars; Beasts and all cattle; Creeping things and flying fowl; Kings of the earth and all peoples; Princes and all judges of the earth; Both young men and maidens; Old men and children.
8. Let them praise the name of the Lord, For His name alone is exalted; His glory is above the earth and heaven.

9. And He has exalted the horn of His people, The praise of all His saints— Of the children of Israel, A people near to Him. Praise the Lord!

PSALM 149
Saints worship the Lord

Worship for salvation (v.1-5).

- Praise the Lord! Sing to the Lord a new song, And His praise in the assembly of saints.
- Let Israel rejoice in their Maker; Let the children of Zion be joyful in their King.
- Let them praise His name with the dance; Let them sing praises to Him with the timbrel and harp.
- For the Lord takes pleasure in His people; He will beautify the humble with salvation.
- Let the saints be joyful in glory; Let them sing aloud on their beds.

Praise for the judgment of God (v.6-9).

Let the high praises of God be in their mouth, and a two-edged sword in their hand, to execute vengeance on the nations, and punishments on the peoples; To bind their kings with chains, and their nobles with fetters of iron; To execute on them the written judgment—This honor have all His saints. Praise the Lord!

PSALM 150
All living creatures praise God

1. Praise the Lord! Praise God in His sanctuary; Praise Him in His mighty firmament!
2. Praise Him for His mighty acts; Praise Him according to His excellent greatness!
3. Praise Him with the sound of the trumpet; Praise Him with the lute and harp!
4. Praise Him with the timbrel and dance; Praise Him with stringed instruments and flutes!
5. Praise Him with loud cymbals; Praise Him with clashing cymbals!
6. Let everything that has breath praise the Lord. Praise the Lord!

This book is called the Song book of Israel by the singer King David. Today most of the believers daily read any one of the psalms to meditate God. It is very simple to understand by any person for their enjoyment in the word of God.